YOU SEE! THERE IS A GOD

Hanna Hofer

YOU SEE! THERE IS A GOD

This book is written to provide information and motivation to readers. Its purpose is not to render any type of psychological, legal, or professional advice of any kind. The content is the sole opinion and expression of the author, and not necessarily that of the publisher.

Copyright © 2024 by Hanna Hofer.

All scriptures are from NKJV

Other books are:
Altars of Remembrance
More Altars of Remembrance
Endless Altars of Remembrance
New Wine
Unworthy but Accepted
A New Vision, it's never too late.

All rights reserved. No part of this book may be reproduced, transmitted, or distributed in any form by any means, including, but not limited to, recording, photocopying, or taking screenshots of parts of the book, without prior written permission from the author or the publisher. Brief quotations for noncommercial purposes, such as book reviews, permitted by Fair Use of the U.S. Copyright Law, are allowed without written permissions, as long as such quotations do not cause damage to the book's commercial value. For permissions, write to the publisher, whose address is stated below.

Printed in the United States of America.

ISBN   978-1-64552-238-6   (Paperback)
ISBN   978-1-64552-237-9   (Digital)

Lettra Press books may be ordered through booksellers or by contacting:

Lettra Press LLC
30 N Gould St. Suite 4753
Sheridan, WY 82801
1 307-200-3414 | info@lettrapress.com
www.lettrapress.com

Contents

Chapter 1	Everything has a reason and was planned	1
Chapter 2	It all had a purpose and a plan	3
Chapter 3	A given time for everything	5
Chapter 4	Another rescue for safety	7
Chapter 5	Was someone in control?	9
Chapter 6	The learning continues	13
Chapter 7	God's help was desperately needed	15
Chapter 8	Always needing His insight and guidance	18
Chapter 9	So many ways to witness	20
Chapter 10	Use what was already given	25
Chapter 11	Longing to know my Lord deeper	28
Chapter 12	The blessed ministry in Juvenile Hall for 35 years	32
Chapter 13	Kayla's fishing angel	36
Chapter 14	The miracles continued	39
Chapter 15	It is such a blessing to be used	43
Chapter 16	The unconditional love of God	46
Chapter 17	This knowledge growth deeper with time	48
Chapter 18	God's word stands forever	50
Chapter 19	Such a valuable gift to us	52
Chapter 20	That precious blood of the Savior	54
Chapter 21	All about our awesome God	56
Chapter 22	And He did plan it all.	58
Chapter 23	Answered prayer	60
Chapter 24	His promises must be taken seriously	62
Chapter 25	His presence can be so near	64

Chapter 26	The awesome blessing of prayer	67
Chapter 27	Believe on Him who justifies	70
Chapter 28	Until the blessed calling	72
Chapter 29	I keep my eye on the finish line	73
Chapter 30	Make your requests out loud	75
Chapter 31	Seek and you will find	76
Chapter 32	There is nothing more precious than time in God's word	78
Chapter 33	Do not worry about what to say	80
Chapter 34	Not the end for witnessing yet	81
Chapter 35	A trip to the San Diego Zoo	83
Chapter 36	Our eternal gratefulness to this Father	85
Chapter 37	A promise made and kept	86
Chapter 38	Still Temptations present	88
Chapter 39	I got the message now	89
Chapter 40	I am still in the works	91
Chapter 41	A new kind of teaching	93
Chapter 42	Relent means to change your mind	94
Chapter 43	One of my miraculous trips in Jordan	95
Chapter 44	Once again, prayer was the answer	97
Chapter 45	The lovely Ukraine	99
Chapter 46	A most awesome promise	101
Chapter 47	One more of the mission trips	103
Chapter 48	The usual emotions displayed	104
Chapter 49	His mercies are new every morning	106
Chapter 50	His promises are to be claimed	108
Chapter 51	Passing on the awesome examples of God	109
Chapter 52	The Big Panorama fire	111
Chapter 53	No end to God's miracles	113
Chapter 54	Our God always takes His word serious	115
Chapter 55	Colorado or bust	117
Chapter 56	Learning about tithing	119
Chapter 57	What you give you get back	121
Chapter 58	Oh the blood of Jesus	123
Chapter 59	Another hip-surgery and the roommates	125

Chapter 60	Sharing the same comfort I received	127
Chapter 61	A God for every situation	129
Chapter 62	My two boy's enlistment	131
Chapter 63	The blessed ministry with my Marines	132
Chapter 64	This became my favorite ministry	133
Chapter 65	Stir up your gift from God	136
Chapter 66	Unlike His creation, only He knows the end	137
Chapter 67	What does meekness mean	139
Chapter 68	Only the Creator knows our new beginning	141
Chapter 69	The good pleasure of His will.	143

1

Everything has a reason and was planned

Not until I was thirty-seven, did this awesome Creator become reality in my life. This was when His eternal bond drew me to Himself as He saved my four children and me. Three years after my husband left us, our Savior began to reveal His gracious plan of Salvation, it was sudden and totally unexpected. When He placed His loving arms around me, it gave me a reason to want to continue living.

Surrendering less often to the enemy was due to the Bible which was given to me. It was God's written word which gave me a wonderful hope for the future, promising me in Jeremiah 29:11 that His plans for me are for good, not evil. This gracious living Lord had planned eternity with Him for my big family and I, that we would spend a life with Him that would never end.

Our God showed us in Romans that 10:17, that the faith He requires comes by hearing and hearing by the word of God. This caused me to increase my time in His life-giving word which lifted my spirit out of depression. His promise to never leave me or forsake me brought a never known peace to my life.

It is a peace that only Jesus can give, and it truly brings joy into the lives of those who seek this loving Savior. I would never have imagine that my life could be one of joy and great adventure, believing as He promises in Matthews 28:11and "lo, I am with you, even to the end of the age,"

When my God showed me Habakkuk 2:2 saying "Write the vision and make it plain on tablets, that he may run who reads it", I knew what He meant. So, I took the notes that I had written after my quiet times and made them into books where I could share my Lords faithfulness.

2

It all had a purpose and a plan.

Well, my new friends, having lived the first eight years of my life in WWII, created in me a real longing for peace. Being raised by a German mom and a Polish dad, gave me an early interest in other countries. Having been told that there is a God in heaven somewhere, who knew about me and punished whenever I did something wrong, made me not want to seek Him.

The war changed our lives in a very negative and painful way, and I never got to see my beloved dad again since I was six. I learned that it was always the innocent people who suffer the most in every war, but prayer was not something that came to our mind in those days. For that we would have had to believe that God existed and cared for us.

However, one night, while hiding again from the bombings in the cellar of my grandparents' apartment building, came a tremendous impact throwing everyone to the ground. It made the ceilings and the walls crumble and shut down all electricity. Thanks to every family having flashlights we all found our way home that night.

The following morning my grandfather took us older children to the backside of the wall we were hiding behind the night before. To our shock there was a tremendous hole in the ground, with a huge black object in it, what we were told was a bomb and it was obvious that this bomb did not explode.

The bomb demolition team chased us away, saying to each other that this monster would have wiped out at least 20 of these apartment buildings. So, we lived with very little help or comfort, everyone just delt with it the best they could as we did also. I never noticed anyone call on God for help.

3

A given time for everything

I could not stop thinking about this incident and for the first time wondered if this could have been God protecting us. Being told that we had to flee because the Russians had entered the east part of Germany forced my mom to grab a few pieces of cloths for the three of us, tied it in towels on our back and tried to catch the last train out of town.

At the end of the day, we were forced out of the train because a bombing was coming, and everyone ran to hide in the forest. My mom was running with us as fast as she could, finally dropping us into a dried-out ditch and herself over us. So, we heard the noises like fireworks but could not see anything.

Our train was destroyed, and another one picked everyone up the next day for the nearest Train Station. We were forced to leave this train also because the last three wagons were needed to pick up some wounded for the Red Cross. My mom handed my sister through the window, woke me up and rushed me to the exit, standing me in the corner of the door.

She pressed her purse into my hand, telling me firmly not to let go and turned to grab my sister Karin, thanking who was holding her. In my sleepiness I let go of the handles in my hand as my mom reached for me to follow the crowd. We had to leave our cloth bundles in order not to be left behind because she had no idea where we were.

My mom discovered that her purse, carrying our only identification papers, was left on the train we had to exit. She rushed to the ticket booth asking the conductor to contact the next station and have her purse taken from the last wagon. She returned crying, sharing that the train we had to get off from had been bombed and everyone on it was killed.

4

Another rescue for safety

Overwhelmed with gratefulness, the thought once again entered my mind, could it have been God who saved our lives again? Being refugees we had to live for three months in a camp, with the mattresses filled with lice. A farmer looking for a worker hired my mom and let us live in an old shack. The ceiling was full of mice, and we had to carefully hide what little food we had.

The bottom floor of the shack was a still and at night it was used to brew alcohol, where men would talk in a bad language till morning. My mom had to work till late hours every day for the farmer who owned the shack we lived in. Having another baby was very hard on my mom but we came to love our sister Magdalena.

One night a fire started after the men had left our shed, and a log must have fallen out of the still, starting a fire. My sisters and I had been overcome by the heavy smoke. Someone shook me roughly and a lady was telling me to wake up, grab my sister Karin and follow her, she had my baby sister and we all got safely outside.

This lady told my mom that she came out from work that night and had a strong urge to take the long way home. Giving in to it, she turned a corner and saw smoke coming out from our shed and knowing my mom was still at work, she came and took us girls out of the burning shed. Once again, the thought of God rescuing us entered my mind. We had been refugees, and it was after two more years when a stream of light entered our lives.

A teacher, who knew my mom from school in her high-school years, found us in that village. He invited us to live on his farm till we found another solution. This was heaven for us girls, regular food, daily schooling and an apple orchard were ours for a while. What Karin and I loved most was spending many after-school hours in those wonderful fruit trees, eating all the apples we wanted.

5

Was someone in control?

My favorite apples were the golden delicious while Karin's were the beautiful red ones. Even though many of the children in those years came down with Polio, the three of us were spared and we all were very grateful. One day my grandma came from far away to visit us and told my mom, since the war was over, to move in with her and grandpa.

Living for the next five years with my mom's parents was not so bad seeing that we were three bombed out refugee families in one apartment with one bathroom. My city was destroyed, including the biggest of all the churches, only one very large wooden cross was left standing there, being counted as a miracle.

Having survived so many hard times and living through them, could it be that this God we heard of was in any way involved? Somehow, we all grew up and having fallen in love with an American soldier, being twenty-one, I followed my husband Bill and our little baby girl to America.

5a   How did I get to that point?

The year of being an exchange student in Switzerland was up for me, and being nineteen years old now, I was headed back home. Having missed my family, my mom and my best friend picked me up from the train station. Gitta introduced me to her fiancé and told me he had a very nice friend and they wanted me to meet him, but I declined, wanting to find a good job first.

However, she brought him anyway, and it took Bill and I two dates to fall in love and we got engaged after three months. Waiting to get married for six months was because the US Army thoroughly checked my background. Bill was in the Army, the 11th Airborne Division, and his three years were up for him to be released. Since I turned out to be three months pregnant, his leaders, not wanting me for eight days on the Ocean, let Bill extend for one more year.

So, we arrived on the famous warship "USS Darby" at the New York Harbor in January 1959. Having to wait for my husband's paperwork, we got to stay in New York five days and went to visit the Statue of Liberty. My husband Bill, being from a city in Southern California, was looking forward to introducing me to his parents.

Being happy that I never got sick those whole eight days on the Ocean, I could take good care of our baby girl Carmelita, calling her Lita. Learning English quickly by a book and tape from the library, I made sure that my in-laws were not talking bad about me. Soon I liked my new country, despite my great homesickness.

This was all a little much for a twenty-one-year-old, but they say love grows wherever it falls and therefore everything worked out splendidly. We lived with his parents during Bills job training and then built our own house on the property next to them. It was a happy marriage and we added three more children, only God had no place in our lives.

5b   A very painful change

My husband Bill loved his job, however after fifteen years he fell in love with a young girl from work and left our four kids and me. Thinking, if there was a God, he was punishing me for not having acknowledged Him all those years, so I would not have run to Him for comfort. However, at my plea, my mom sold her home and belongings and followed me with my 18-year-old sister to the USA.

Our favorite fragrance of gingerbread was once again filling the home and brought memories of Christmases past. My two daughters, Lita and Chris, were taking out the batch of cookies from the oven to replace it with the next sheet. The boys, Stephen, and Billy, got to play with the wooden and cloth ornaments, I did not trust them with the glass ones yet.

Suddenly, with deep pain, I realized that for the first time in fifteen years my husband would not spend Christmas with us. Walking to the closet for more ornaments kept my kids from seeing my tears but it made this holiday a painful memory. Earlier that year my husband had walked up to me and said that he wanted a divorce and walked out the door.

Almost three-year-old Stephen noticed that his dad did not close the door all the way, so he got out and ran after his dad wanting a ride. My still being frozen at the same spot, His dad shoved his son back in and closed the door securely this time. Not being able to tell my teenage daughters for two days why Daddy was not home anymore made me feel depressed.

When I was finally able to tell my girls about their dad being gone, one of their responses was to quit school and stay away from home. They told me later they were hoping Dad would look for them and come back home. The next three years were the most painful of my life. It hurt so bad because there was nothing I could do for my girls, so depression increased, and I started to drink which added hangovers the next day.

But that was still better than the pills the doctor had given me, those pills just removed any feelings and emotions. My oldest daughter and her friends had taken my car for a joyride and totaled it, making me lose my job. Not finding any help, I tried to start drinking again, but for some reason the alcohol tasted disgusting, so I left it alone.

5c   A beautiful turn for our lives

So, on a very hot mid-July day I took an old make-up kit and headed for an assigned territory I had been given. At the first door a lady answered, she asked me in and offered me a glass of cold water because of the heat. Telling her why I was on foot, she asked if I would like to turn my problem over to the Lord, to which I had to admit to not knowing what she was talking about.

She said her name was Donna and that she had just moved to California, being on staff with a Ministry called Campus Crusade for Christ. Telling her I was on foot because I had just lost my car and job, *and she asked if I would like to give this problem to the Lord. Admitting not knowing what she was talking about, she pulled out a small yellow booklet, and asked if she could share it with me.*

The title was "Do you know the four spiritual laws" and she said it would show me how to become a Christian. For some strange reason I was interested, and it began "God loves you and has a wonderful plan for your life." Considering my current circumstances, I really wanted to know more, and she continued. When we got to the prayer to ask Jesus into my heart I was weeping and truly meant what it said.

I remember a peace coming over me and I agreed to her visiting me to teach me more. We forgot all about my selling her make-up and I hugged the Bible she gave me, the first one I ever had. My depression seemed to be gone and I felt like I arrived at home in no time, and I spent most of my days reading God's wonderful word.

Imagining that God would give me, a sinner, a chance to receive His only son, and that He would want to live in me brought real joy, the first I had in a long time. With tears I hung on to every word as Donna showed me what happened to me and Whom I now belonged to forever. It seemed so unusual that I trusted what this Bible taught, but for some reason I knew this was the truth.

My beginning to read the Bible was in July of 1974, a gracious and merciful God convinced me that He exists and has chosen this time for my Salvation. Having lost my job, I put out resumes everywhere possible but had no replies. Coming home one day, I dropped on a chair, asking my Savior why He has not found me a job.

Suddenly the phone rang, and the voice said this is Campus Crusade for Christ and the man asked if I am still looking for a fulltime job. When I answered yes, he asked if I could report Monday morning in accounting. Taking a deep breath, I asked my heavenly Father, what will I do in accounting, I am a medical assistant?

6

The learning continues

Well, I started in accounting and after some good teaching, I began to like it. However, after five years my gracious Lord moved me to "Donor Relations", and I loved it. This enabled me to report God's work, being done by our staff in every country, to the donors on my caseload. Caseload meant this group of people were only to be contacted by me.

They loved these reports and were grateful for my calls, which kept my spirit always high. The only sad situation in my life was that my two daughters had not received the Savior, this God who loved them, into their hearts yet. Bringing them in prayer to my Lord was the greatest desire of my heart and lifting them before His presence became my daily joy.

Using Isaiah 55:11 which says, "so is My word that comes from My mouth, it will not return to me empty, but it will accomplish what I please and will prosper in what I send it to do." I realized that what He sends His word for, is Salvation. So, I prayed that scripture many times a day and this beloved Lord answered in a special way.

At one of my Bible studies with Diana, not only my girls were home for it, but also their boyfriends. I said a quick prayer, took a deep breath and went into the kitchen to make an important request. To my overwhelming joy, not only did they agree to want Jesus in their hearts but all four wanted to be baptized. You can imagine the gratefulness of this mom to her merciful Savior God.

My mornings were now spent getting my kids off to school and then sitting on my couch and reading my heavenly Father's word. I truly saw that He loved me, and He continued teaching me, using the love letter He wrote to His children. My two sons were raised in the knowledge of their Lord from an early age and grew up following Him with me.

7

God's help was desperately needed

One day my daughter Lita came home to tell me that her dad was going to marry his current girlfriend and apply for half custody of our two boys. My blood drained from my face for a moment, but I immediately called out my heavenly Father's name asking for His wisdom and peace.

My heart ached for them, they were only seven and nine and it scared me to think how confusing their lives would be now. We had Bible studies every day, we never missed church the three times a week or the AWANA youth programs, so the Lord had truly blessed this.

However, I knew what to do and reached for my Bible, which was always nearby. While talking with the Lord my Bible had fallen open and looking down, my eyes fell on Isaiah 54:4-10 telling me "Fear not for you will not be ashamed, neither be disgraced, for you will not be put to shame, for you will forget the shame of your youth and will not remember the reproach of your widowhood anymore."

> *Then it continued, "For your Maker is your husband, the Lord of hosts is His name, and your Redeemer is the Holy One of Israel, He is called the God of the whole earth. For the Lord has called you like a woman forsaken and grieved in spirit, like a youthful wife when you were refused," says your God.*

> *And verse 13 goes on "All your children shall be taught by the Lord and great shall be the peace of your children." Then my Savior*

finishes in verse 17," No weapon formed against you shall prosper, and every tongue which rises against you in judgement You shall condemn." I thought at first this was only written for Israel, but then it ends with "This is the heritage of the servants of Lord, and their righteousness is from Me," says the Lord.

There was an overwhelming peace that flooded my heart and soul because I was sure that I was His servant. It was four days later when I got a message from Bill's mother that he had had a stroke and was totally paralyzed on the left side of his body. We were not allowed to see him until two days later and even then, he stayed in a coma. The doctor said that he could hear us, so we kept telling him about our growth in the Lord.

7a A new hope for the future.

One day I received a letter from the cities Rehabilitation Center, offering me fulltime college classes plus free childcare. They said I was eligible because of my hip replacements that were needed for me to walk without a limp again. My choice was Medical Assistant because that was my job before I got married.

They chose a well-known business college for my classes and San Bernardino Hospital for my on-the-job training. My routine was very busy, and I told the kids that this would be only for a year, then there would be a good job. This would mean we have some money to go some places especially the beach we loved.

My girls did not trust my promises, I had made many and had to cancel most of them. I had been told God is a strong ruler whom you obey or there would be no mercy. In order to get into heaven my good list will have to be longer than my bad list or I would be left out. Being pretty sure that my good list was not longer, kept me from seeking Him. Not having been in church since childhood I figured my husbands leaving was God's punishment.

Finally meeting a nice gentleman seemed a perfect solution to my loneliness. It was so nice to receive roses, be told I am lovely and great to be with, healed much of the past hurts. I continued dating him until he proposed marriage, at which time I had to be honest with him. It was not fair to him that I saw him because I needed him, however I did not love him.

Telling him was not easy but it was the truth, and it was a sad farewell, even for my kids.

8

Always needing His insight and guidance.

The story of Bill, the father of my children, has a good ending, thanks to the mercy of God. Three days before our son Steve left for the Army, he and his brother Bill took their father fishing in his wheelchair to witness to him one more time. About noontime I got a call at work from Steve saying, Mom, the kingdom has a new member, our dad. We praised our God and Steve could leave for Korea with the Army in peace.

With all the best teaching, at times I still fell for Satan's accusations. That was before a Christian brother gave his testimony at our devotion time at work. Having had the same problem with guilt, the Savior showed him that it is the blood of Jesus that washed our sins white as snow, and removed them forever. One time in Hebrews 8:12 He declares "I will be merciful to their unrighteousness, and their sins and their lawless deeds I will remember no more."

The scriptures tell us to bring up that precious blood often because it reminds the enemy that it is the blood of the lamb that defeated him for all times. The Savior tells us in Hebrews 10:14 "For by one offering He has <u>perfected forever</u> those who are being sanctified." Everything my beloved God does is perfect, and I did not know some of the reasons till later.

In 1993, Campus Crusade had me ordained while volunteering in the city's Youth Detention Center called Juvenile Hall. All my teaching hours were in the evenings, after work, and Sunday mornings to give a Service from eight to nine. When I found out they had visiting times on Saturday and Sunday afternoon, I volunteered then also because no one waited for me at home anymore.

This became a very meaningful ministry the Lord had put me in because it also helped me with the pain of my empty nest. My two daughters were married by then and my two sons had joined the Service. After coming to know these young prisoners, a few became special, and I help them in whatever possible ways. This was such a satisfaction to a mother who was temporarily separated from her kids.

Probation did not permit contact with their inmates after they were released unless the contact person was ordained or on staff. So, I took on the year and six-month training and Campus Crusade for Christ had me ordained and I have a lifetime membership, renewed every year. It is a lovely opportunity to marry, baptize or give a memorial service. I have met many lovely people this way and told them about this awesome God of love.

9

So many ways to witness

One special event I want to share, regarding the ordination, it involved a special Christian friend. She was my oldest daughter's mother-in-law, who enjoyed the Savior with me. This special sister in Christ, her name is Christina, got cancer and we got in much prayer before she went to be home with our Lord. Missing her caused her son to spend more time at my house and we searched the Bible for many comforting scriptures.

Her husband knew about my being an ordained minister and asked me if I would please perform the memorial service. Loving my friend, and her son being my son in law, I wholeheartedly agreed. I made sure that the Salvation plan was shared so the participants knew there was a way to see her again someday. This was a great chance to mention this wonderful Savior who gave His life so His followers could spend a beautiful everlasting life with Him.

My friend's son, being a strong believer by now, told me that several of the participants were deeply touched by God's message. We could not tell if my friend's husband received Jesus Christ as Savior, but he kept mentioning all afternoon how much he enjoyed the message. It was a blessing for me to be a part of my dear friends homegoing and have the comfort of seeing her in eternity again. I will continue praying for my friend's husband till his Salvation is confirmed.

It also was a great joy when my youngest son and his wife wanted to renew their wedding vows after 10 years and asked me to officiate the ceremony in the name of Jesus. Also, my oldest grandson and his bride asked me to perform their wedding ceremony. The bride being Filipino, they wanted half the food to be Filipino and half Bavarian. My grandson wanted the same Bavarian meal we enjoyed every Christmas eve together.

There is nothing as meaningful as knowing that this powerful loving Lord is in control of everything in life and at the end welcomes His beloved children home. It is a deep longing for me to lead as many as possible into the arms of this merciful and forgiving Creator. He gives them an amount of faith and the Holy Spirit, so they will continue to seek Him. I experienced that myself when I first came to know Him. This was the only reason I had such a hunger for the Bible.

9a   The growing continues

When God loving me became hard to believe, Donna pointed me to the Scriptures and showed me that my God wanted me a I was. It explained that the cleanup of my life had to be His, not mine. It was amazing to me, and I was grateful for it. My mornings were now spent feeding my kids, sending them off to school and reeding my Bible.

Weeping over the things He was telling me showed me more and more how truly He loved me. One of the favorite in His Word was and is, Romans 8:38 and 39, were He says rhat no one and nothing can separate me from His love, not even Angels or Demons. He also promises in John 10:27 – 31 that no one can snatch me out of His or the Father's hand because He and the Father are One.

Reading God's word daily began to really change my life and I loved Him more each time. The first gift for reading His Word was my mother-in-law. She strongly disliked me and displayed that whenever her son was absent. This was hard because we lived with her during the years of my husband's job training.

When my Bible reading began, her dislike suddenly changed, and she became friendly. Our neighbors even shared with me how happy she was that I married her son and that I was a good mother to my girls. Some miracles also happened with my boys whose grades began going up and the relations with their teachers greatly improved.

Though I accepted His word regarding the washing away of my sins, Satan was furious at having lost me. This enemy tried to attack me with guilt due to the still unhappy lives of my two daughters. Guilt seems to be one of Satan's greatest weapons for discouraging God's beloved children. However, He tells us that if we refuse Satan, he will flee, which brought great relieve and wisdom.

9b   When storm clouds arise

There was a time when I realized that there might be trouble coming my way and I got the faithful consultant, my Bible. I asked my beloved Lord for insight and His words in my mouth. His life-giving word always has the right advice, if I ask for it and then follow it. It came strongly to my mind to use Paul's trip to Rome on a ship in Acts 27, being hit by a storm. It is a great example to use for our own lives in the way everyone on board responded to Paul's advice he received from the Lord.

Visiting the church of a friend, her pastor suggested when in trouble, check where I go for advice. So, I went back to my Creator and began to read the story in Acts 27. If a storm hit a relationship, my job or health, His word clarified the results quickly. Even though Paul advised against the trip at this time of the year because of the bad weather, no one listened. Tossing everything unnecessary overboard did not help anything, neither did the wiring together nor patch up of the boat.

Having been in a situation where nothing could be improved, I ran for God's word. Is it not wonderful that I was invited to come to my Savior at times like that and say "help, only you can fix this." If I left it to Him, He picked it up and in His perfect will restored it to what it should have been in the first place. He said in Romans 8:28 that we know that all things work together for good to those who love God, to those who are the called according to His purpose.

He will continue His beautiful work of making me into the person He always wanted me to be. This is what this God of love offers to everyone, it just needs to be accepted and used. To love Him means to know Him, and the only way that will happen is with much time in the letter He wrote to His children. That is what we need to live this Christian life and to honor

Him. He loves His children so deeply; nothing is too much for Him to give them and to have them eternally with Him.

Jesus gave the biggest gift of all, His life, and all He wanted in return was our heart and our obedience. All the rules and do and don't for salvation were added by the leaders not by the Savior. Being in His precious word daily, taught me how to live and love after I was His and He had given me the Holy Spirit and grace to follow the instructions how to live a holy life.

9c   His promises are always true

Remembering that He knew me before creation, I looked up Ephesians 1:4 and 5 for reference. It says that the Father chose us in Jesus before He laid the foundation of the world. This was so we would be holy and without blame before Him in love. He had already predestined us to adoption as sons by Jesus Christ to Himself, according to the good pleasure of His will.

Our beloved merciful Creator knew we would mess up, yet He created us anyway. He also knew that He would finish the work He began in us but not until it was time. This blessed work was not to be finished until He was ready to take us home to be wi th Him forever. This gracious Savior never tires of inviting us to come to Him because we are already forgiven, and He will help us to stay on the right road.

Violent storms bring hopelessness, and the self-effort of Paul's companions   could not keep the boat from breaking up. Christians easily bail out when things at their meeting place do not agree with them and find another place to worship. It is important to our Father to love and support the Church body He has led us to, and be agreeable and try to work out changes to their place of worship.

Paul was instructed to tell the sailors that only those on the boat would be saved, so they stayed. This would not be the time to leave the marriage, or job or the doctor, this was the time to trust once again the One who saved us and called us. The outcome will amaze us because our great God always does His very best because all things are possible to Him.

He says in Romans 8:32,33, "He who did not spare His own son but delivered Him up for us all, how shall He not with Him also freely give us all things. Who shall bring a charge against God's elect? It is God who justifies." I cannot even imagine this kind of generosity; I will be grateful for all eternity and try to be obedient to His commands.

10

Use what was already given

Taking some bread, Paul encouraged everyone to take what God had already provided, gave thanks and all partook and felt encouraged. This is a time that He makes us stronger, and we trust Him even more and wait for His best. It sometimes takes a while, but God never lets His beloved children down, but always has His perfect timing.

In my life God had wisdom provided in a person, but I was not aware of it, being too busy feeling sorry for myself. Searching my heart and seeing what my Creator has done lately and thank Him and I used it wisely. Now I try more to be aware of what this Savior has provided for me instead of following my own ideas.

There is not much left now but there comes a time in the storm when we have to cut loose from what we have trusted in and grab a board and surf to shore. Our Lord promised in Romans 8:28 "And we know that all things work together for good to those who love God, those who are the called according to His purpose." We can always lean on Him and be safe in His outstretched arms which are continuously waiting for us.

When daytime arrived, our sailors could not see the land and decided to drive the ship against the cliff as far as they could. Cutting off the anchors and loosening the rudders, they let the boat drift till it broke up in the sea and they headed for the beach on whatever they could grab. They did not have much to get them there, but this was what God had provided.

This is the first-time bodyboarding was created and our wise God never runs out of ideas as he does not for us either. If we ignore God's warnings our storms are tough. However, if we listen to His warnings, and take His provisions, He promises to see us through. He never promised to remove the trials, He only promises us to be in them with us and see us through.

10a   I have called you by your name, you are Mine.

The Lord tells us in Isaiah verses 1& 2 "This is what the Lord says, the One who created you Jacob, and the One who formed you Israel, "Do not fear for I have redeemed you; I have called you by your name, you are Mine. I will be with you when you pass through the waters and when you pass through the rivers, they will not overwhelm you. You will not be scorched when you walk through the fire, and the flame will not burn you."

Wow, this is only one of the thousands of my beloved Father's promises, it makes me want to love and follow Him with all my heart. There is no one in my life that can love me and protect me like this awesome Creator and Redeemer. There is no one who could be with me every moment of my life and promise me that no one and nothing can ever separate me from His love, promised in Romans 8:38 and 39.

His precious word tells me that I am part of Israel because He has grafted me into the True Vine when I became His. That beautiful story of the True Vine is so clearly explained in John chapter 15:1-5. It explains that Jesus is the Vine and His believers are the branches being prepared to live In His kingdom forever. He continues in verse 5," He who abides in Me and I in him, bears much fruit, for without Me you can do nothing."

> Yet in Philippians 4:13 He promises "I can do all things through Christ who strengthens me." This shows that the difference is being in Christ, and all things will be possible, and we will bear much fruit. This is such a powerful promise and means that everybody can do this according to Galatians

3:27-28, "For as many of you were baptized into Christ you have put on Christ. There is neither Jew nor Greek, there is neither Slave nor free, there is neither male nor female, for you are all one in Chris Jesus."

If we are one in Him, living in His kingdom will be more beautiful than we can imagine. Getting ready to live in His kingdom seems the most important goal in this present life. To follow the instructions is not that hard because they are very clear. It depends on the willingness to obey them and receive the blessings and rewards promised in keeping them. Longing to live with my generous and loving God forever is a very good incentive to be in His instructive Word as much as possible.

11

Longing to know my Lord deeper

During an evening Bible study, I was aware of wanting to know my beloved God in a deeper way. So, I began to spend more time in His life-giving word and am keeping my Bible on my bed now. One morning I was in Isaiah 58 and read a teaching that totally fascinated me even though I had read it before. It was all about the kind of fasting that pleases the Lord.

Starting with verse seven, where it says, "Is it not to share your bread with the hungry, and that you bring to your house the poor who are cast out, when you see the naked that you cover him and not hide yourself from your own flesh." It meant to me to be helpful whenever the chance arises, and I was very grateful that the Lord had given me the chances and helped me to be obedient.

One of these chances of taking someone in who had been cast out was thirteen years ago and she is still living with me today. I got to feed her and pay for her utilities, and she got to use my car till she got a job. This also covered not hiding myself from my flesh, because this was a relative. For my obedience my beloved God has blessed my ministries and has increased them giving me an additional chance with youths.

Having spent more time with my beloved bridegroom Jesus in His lifechanging letter, has increased my love and trust for Him. I should remember that it is also how it works in human relationships. The more I want to know and trust someone the more meaningful time I need to devote to that person. This is how it was in my marriage, which lasted fifteen years and then fell apart because Bill and I let God have no part in it.

Bill was a good husband and father but when temptations came, he had no one to draw strength and wisdom from and so just left his family. Thanks be to God, a month before the Lord took him home with another stroke, he received Jesus as his Lord and Savior. It happened through our oldest son Steve, three days before Steve left for Korea in the Army. This was one of so many endless ways our Creator showed us His never-ending faithfulness.

11a   Standing on His promises

There were times when I had to truly stand on my Savior's promises, not my feelings. Remembering that Jesus Christ said He came so we would have an abundant life, right here and now. I began to believe it and claimed it as well.

This promise I made invalid by allowing the enemy to throw me into doubt every time my Lord's work did not make sense to me. Trusting Him completely still needed more work of me surrendering everything into His capable hands. But even more, leaving it there.

My daughter Chris was to meet with her manager one afternoon and I waited at Lita's home in case Chris needed me that night. Little Christopher was with me so I could take him to her when she was done. When we had not heard from Chris by eight pm, I inquired at her job. I was told that she had been terminated and left work over an hour ago.

Asking the Lord to keep my heart and mind still, and acknowledging that He knew exactly her whereabouts, I gave thanks to my Lord by faith. Surely, He had shown me His great faithfulness by now and I would be able to trust Him. It was time to drive home because the baby had to be in bed.

The ringing of the phone startled me, it being after one am, and answering sleepily, I realized it was Chris. She was crying, telling me that this was more than she could handle with her husband having left the two of them. She could not go on like this unless the Lord would help her out in this.

11b   What this God has done for one He will do for all, if asked.

Amazed at the calmness of my heart, I assured her that this loving Creator knew all about her problems. Reminding her of my similar situation and crying out to my Savior, how He took care of everything, she calmed down. He also promises that he who calls on the name of the Lord shall be saved and again, he who comes to Him will in o way will be cast out.

I closed by assuring her that He says He never lies, and it tells us in Proverbs 18:10 that the name of the Lord is a strong tower, the righteous run to it and are saved. Chris sounded calm by now and asked me if I would keep Christopher till morning she would be at my house to pick him up.

Now the only thing for me to do was place this child of mine back into the outstretched of this beloved Savior's arms, keeping my heart open before Him. Oh, how good it is to know that He takes care of all we entrust to Him, especially our children. He tells us in Psalms 46:10, to cease striving and know that He is God.

The next morning my mom was having breakfast with me and expected me to be as worried about Chris as she was. Describing to her that my peace comes from knowing that our God loves Chris so much. He longs to reveal that love to her and can show this in her current circumstances that her enemy brought to her.

So working this out had to be in the Lord's hand and not mine, an working it out He truly did. Two days after this, Chris's problems were taken care of. She did not have to leave her apartment and got an offer for a much better job. Chris was more at peace after this and began to trust this God she was coming to know.

11c The strong meaning of being sealed

The first time I read in the Bible about being sealed I studied it often and found all the scriptures that had this subject. My favorite ones I wrote down quickly so I would not forget the promises. It is Ephesian 1:13 which states "In Him you also trusted, after you heard the word of truth, the gospel of your salvation, in whom also, having believed, you were sealed with the Holy Spirit of promise.

There was something so final, so permanent about it, like no one can ever take it away from me, I am forever His. Another one is in 2 Corinthians 5:5 saying, "Now He who has prepared us for this very thing is God, who also has given us the Spirit as a guarantee." So, we know that while we are at home in the body, we are still physically absent from the Lord.

A seal is an identifying mark placed on an important official document or contract and it always shows who it belongs to. God put His seal on those that have received Him as Savior and Lord for all eternity, never to be lost or alone again. Satan will try to persuade us that this is not real or that we can lose it.

However, my Savior promises in Romans 8:38 and 39 saying "I am persuaded that neither death nor life, nor angels nor principalities nor powers, nor things present nor things to come, nor height nor depth, nor any other created thing, shall be able to separate us from the love of God which is in Christ Jesus our Lord."

WOW, I don't think there is any more powerful promise in my Fathers love letter to His children.

12

The blessed ministry in Juvenile Hall for 35 years

What a joy to see my first grandchildren grow up around me and know I will take any opportunity to teach them about the Lord. When my Savior wanted me in ministry, He had a neighbor invite me to a meeting at the city's Youth Detention Center. She knew from church that I loved teaching high schoolers and thought this would be the perfect spot for me.

At one of our meetings one of the Bible teachers was moving away and asked if I would please take over his unit. Even though I did not know what to expect, I really wanted to minister to these young troublemakers. Trying to imagine what their young lives may have experienced, and what they have been through so far, I wanted them to meet their awesome Creator.

Desiring to introduce these students and show them this loving and trustworthy God, I knew the Lord helped me greatly with the writing of the Bible lessons. I started out with one Unit and ended up with five of the Units because I was asked if I was willing to take other units as their teachers left. The chaplain asked for me to take additional Units till they could find a replacement, but they never did find any, and did not look.

This was fine with me because no one was waiting for me at home and the thirty-five years there became a very fulfilling part of my life. I still have my first two note books with all their names and crosses, which explain their salvations. Whenever one prayed to received Jesus as their Savior, he got to draw a cross by his name. This helped me to pray for each of them accordingly.

There was a time when one of my students, I will call him Kevin, having been transferred, with two from another Unit to a Center in Nevada. This place had a big frozen lake and the three of them went for some fun. One of them, going out unto the lake broke through the ice and began to yell for help. Both his friends went out to help him, but all three of them drowned.

His director called to tell me so I would be prepared when I came for that evenings Bible study. Knowing about my book with the names and crosses, he asked me to please check if his name had a cross next to it. Being in tears I could tell him "yes" and gratefully his whole Unit clapped, and we thanked the Savior that we will get to see him again.

12 Dearly loved Arrowhead Springs

My first seventeen years were working in the beautiful Arrowhead Springs Hotel in the foothills of the San Bernardino mountains. There is no way to describe my joy of driving up and down the hill every day going past those ancient pine trees leading up to the entrance. This Hotel is located directly below an enormous natural Arrowhead carved by nature on the face of the mountain.

This mountain is behind the Hotel and the Arrowhead points down to the beautiful 300 room all white buildings. It is surrounded by the big trees of this national park and looks like out of a fairytale. The Hotel has a very fascinating history, especially because of the very hot waters under its grounds. On the weekends I would have my family up for blessed and fun times.

Often I would dance in the water, holding one of my little ones and sing "Jesus loves me this I know" to them. After work each summer I would go home, pick up my children, made cool aid and peanut butter sandwiches and go back up to swim. That was after we first went to the natural steam caves that were underground do to the 93% hot water.

This Hotel was very popular in Hollywood because some of the famous actors spent their vacations there. Those beautiful grounds also have a spectacular Olympic size pool where some of the "Esther William's" movies were filmed. It contains an indoor as well as an outdoor theater.

Dr Bill Bright purchased this Hotel and properties in 1961 to use as headquarters for a fast-growing international ministry he had started in Hollywood. This is also where I started the first 17 of 47 years of my job with this blessed ministry and some awesome training. My two sons and I had the joy of swimming many summer days in that lovely pool.

These were unforgettable years of blessings and coming to know an unimaginably loving and merciful Creator. I never had thought this God I came to know would make such a change in my life and that of my children. They never stopped believing as it said in the sign over our front door, "As for me and my house, we will serve the Lord." The sign remains there today.

12   Forgiveness, a great release

One of the things the Lord kept putting in my mind was to have a closer relationship with Him. This could only happen by my heart being free of any unforgiveness against people who had hurt me. Knowing my past, the lady who had led me to the Lord paid for me to attend a famous Bill Gothard seminar. It was all about forgiveness and so she offered to watch my boys for me.

Attending fully convinced me that this was what my Savior wanted me to do and I agreed. He persuaded me to start with the hardest one, which was my children's father. Starting to dial several times, I was hoping he would not answer, but he did. Asking Bill to forgive me for whatever part I had in him losing his love for me was hard.

Flippantly he said "ok, I forgive you." Hanging up the phone, anger arose in me saying "who forgives who here"? However, as soon as the thought came, I had to ask the Lord to forgive me. This was the beginning of a whole new freedom because I was obedient to my beloved Father and the blessing would come.

Forgiveness became an important part of my life as I learned that my forgiving was for my own relief and freedom, whether the other person said yes or no. Having done my part freed me from that situation and gave me the peace my Savior died for me to have, it soon released it to my unconscious mind where it belonged.

The Lord promises in Jeremiah 29:11 "I know the plans I have for you," says the Lord, "they are plans for good not evil, to give you a future and a hope." This helps me not to worry about what lies ahead because I can trust Him, He never lies. He wrote everything about it in His precious letter to His children.

12a   Awesome protection in a rainstorm

In 2007 my youngest son Bill and his wife moved his family to Kentucky, where her parents followed them. It was hard from seeing them almost daily to seeing them once a year. Getting to Kentucky and visiting once a year became a treasured habit and once again it was time for farewell.

Bill loaded up my luggage and usually the whole family comes to the Airport with us. However, this time it was cold and rainy, so they stayed home. Leaving a little earlier than usual because we had to drive slower, it poured by the time we got to Lexington.

Getting ready to turn left, being on the outside of three lanes, we were ready to turn with the others. We were almost finished turning when our car suddenly shot ahead sliding fast. This is so hard to explain, I hope you can follow my picture.

So, our car slit in front of the two lanes next to us, over a large cement street divider and into the oncoming traffic on the other side of the street . Holding my eyes closed, calling out my Saviors name, expecting one of those many cars to hit us, our car suddenly stopped.

Opening my eyes, I was in total surprise, our car had stopped in the left turning lane of the opposite side of the street. Bill and I hugged and thanked our beloved Protector, and I still had enough time not to miss my flight. It is such a blessing and joy to experience our God watching over those He loves.

Even in strange or risky situations, if I make myself aware of it, I can feel His presence and get peace. Jesus said so clearly in John 14:18, "I will not leave you orphans, I will come to you." However, after He had risen from the dead, He no longer had to come to us, because He lives in us and we can just begin to speak with Him.. Hallelujah!

13

Kayla's fishing angel

One thing my children, grandchildren and great grandchildren all like is fishing. Taking them up the mountains every Saturday had become a great joy to me. One of those days my oldest daughter Lita, three of her grandchildren and I went up to the lake for some fishing. Having had a foot injury, I did not walk to their favorite fishing spot with them this time.

On the south side of the lake, where a large parking lot was, the lake had a long wall to retain that side of the water. It looked like fun to play in, however, it was packed thick with seaweed. Explaining to the girls that the danger of falling in was that it would be impossible to swim, due to the weeds winding around their legs. This would also prevent anyone to swim in and rescue them.

So, off they went to see what they can catch and returned about two hours later with a few fish. Lita and two of the girls decided to go home and packed up their car, as everyone else seemed to be doing because it was Sunday night. Kayla and I wanted to stay a little longer so no one else was left at the lake except the two of us and one little lady sitting on a bench.

Kayla had given this lady and a few others one of our Christian witnessing booklets before they went to go fishing. Since my girl was the last to return, I started to close up my paints when suddenly I heard a yelp and Kayla was gone. In spite of my injury, I ran as fast as I could asking our God for help, knowing that my arms were not long enough to reach my eight-year-old.

When I reached the lake, due to a great miracle Kayla was not in the water but on a small pile of gravel against the wall. I realized that even though I was 5'7, my arms would not be long enough to reach my great granddaughter. Suddenly that little lady from the bench was next to me and with one swift pull had Kayla at my side. My girl and I hugged and turned to thank that precious lady but there was not one person anywhere. All the beach goers had left because it was Sunday evening and following was a workday.

When Kayla and I looked back down we saw that her fishing pole had drifted a little away, due to the waves. However, to our great amazement, the small pile of gravel she had stood on was no longer there. With grateful hearts we acknowledged our Lords intervention. When I told my family the whole story, they rejoiced also and thanked God with us for the angel.

13a   My sister Magdalena

We called my youngest sister Maggie, she too had married an Army man, they had three children and lived in Houston, Texas. While her husband was away on tour of duty, she and the girls came to stay with my mom for a month. They were also on my daily prayer list, and I had asked my Savior to give me a chance to share with them His plan of Salvation.

Well true to our faithful God, their chance came in the first week being with us. My mom paid for us to spend three days in a lovely cabin in the San Bernardino mountains. One day while Maggie was taking a nap, the girls and I took a walk. Strolling through the beautiful forest we sat on a large wooden log and the Holy Spirit whispered, "an open-door Hannah".

Getting the message, I began asking the girls if they knew the story about Jesus and at their no, I began to explain. It was a joy to me that they listened intently as I began to reveal Jesus' love, which He had for them before they were born. Telling them that He knew them before He made the world and already picked them to be His own.

When all three agreed to ask Jesus to be their Savior, we prayed the salvation prayer and hugged because we were sisters forever now. Promising them Bibles they were really happy, but not as happy as this aunt who got more of her prayers answered. My chance with my sister Maggie came two days later and to my surprise she also listened intently without questioning any of what she heard. She also received Jesus as her Lord and said she had seen the peace in my live and wanted that also.

We all rejoiced and celebrated with a nice dinner for being now together in a special family and agreed to pray for Dad to come to that decision also. I stayed in close touch with them, wanting to be sure they would not walk away from what they had learned.

14

The miracles continued

It was a very emotional farewell and my sister and I, promised to see each other more often now. The next day Maggie called me and shared a miracle with me. Before she boarded the plane, she asked the Lord to take away her smoking habit, which she tried to quit all her adult life. As she continued, she began to cry, telling me that when she left the plane, she expected to light up a cigarette but found that she had lost all desire.

Even the rest of the day and this next week, there was a bad taste in her mouth when she thought about having a smoke. When I called her two weeks later, she said that she was so grateful to the Lord who loved her so much that He took away a habit she picked up when she was sixteen. It was a joy to me that she knew whom to thank.

There were times when I had to stand on my Saviors promises and not on my feelings. Remembering that Jesus said He came that we would have an abundant life right here on earth I began to believe it and claimed it as well. These promises I repeated whenever I allowed the enemy to throw me into doubt or worry.

The growth continued by increasing my time in my Father's love letter, as He revealed His will for me a little more with each search. It has been a joy to talk with my sister because she enjoys whatever spiritual subject I bring up and does not get tired of it. It is such a blessing to know that all the ones I have been praying for will be with me in that flight to heaven, not because of what I have done but what their Savior did.

My beloved mom and two years later my sister Karin went to be with the Lord due to cancer. It was such a privilege and honor to be with them almost daily and fill them with God's blessed word, assuring them of His hopeful promises. They both left peacefully in their sleep waiting like the rest of us for a reunion in heaven.

14a   The fire at our house

One day my daughter Lita called, saying that one of the tires burst on their car and asked if they could borrow my spare. Stephen and our puppy were sleeping, and they were only two streets over from me, so I took Billy and rushed off. Lita's husband Raymond was almost done when we saw two fire trucks pass by us. Lita and I left to see where the trucks went to and were shocked when they not only turned into our street but had stopped at our house.

To my great relieve Stephen and the puppy came running towards us and we pulled over. While we watched the fire being contained, I was so amazed at the total peace that filled my mind and heart. My having experienced our God's faithfulness at earlier times caused me to trust Him, instead of falling apart. So now, in my first big trial since our Lord saved us, I was sure all would be well.

There was nothing left of the garage or any ceiling or roof in the house except over the three back bedrooms. So, we gathered and took whatever we could carry, and which was not damaged by the fire, and spent the first two days with my in-laws.

Calling our friend Donna, she told me she would ask Campus Crusade about us staying at the Arrowhead Springs Hotel until my insurance had a place for us. There were actually seven of us at this time because my son-in-law had lost his job and they had no place to live, so the four of them moved in with us. We were very grateful when Campus Crusade allowed us to stay in the dorms and would even provide our meals.

Visiting our house the next day, we noticed that the fire had gone exactly to where the cracks in the ceilings had ended. It took me a few minutes to realize that our awesome God had stopped the fire smack-dab where the damage had ended. Being grateful to our generous Provider would have been an understatement because our entire roof and ceiling on the house would be replaced.

14b   The Lord's never ending grace

The Insurance agent however, showed me on the insurance papers that the only part of the house covered was the structure. This meant that everything else was at our own cost, even the terribly damaged carpet throughout our home. I notified our prayer team and friends, and we went to prayer. So, needless to say, that prayer once again worked, and our beloved God had everything in the house replaced.

The end of November, my neighbor told me that their insurance company had their entire house cleaned because of the smoke damage. This would be nice for ours also, especially since it was for sale due to our move to Colorado. The smoke damage was still there but I did not want to make another claim, I was so grateful for what they had already done.

A week later two men came to our door and showed their IDs for being with my insurance company. Asking their intention, they stated that they were cleaning many homes in my neighborhood for smoke damage and ours was included. They looked in all the rooms and informed me, if I agreed, they would get rid of that smoke odor.

We informed them that we had already cleaned up all the sand and ashes on the windows and curtains but would be grateful for their help. They said a refund check would be coming for our work which they would have had to pay for another crew. The next day men arrived and shampooed the carpets and upholstery and said the painters would come the next day.

Our Christmas was very special this year because we had learned to truly thank our beloved God for His incredible gift, His son Jesus Christ. For the first time the gifts had less value than the precious one given by our heavenly Father.

Stephen and Billy were to be picked up by their dad and his girlfriend for a few hours and they prayed for a chance to witness to him again. When the boys were dropped off, they had received presents but what they wanted most did not happen. Assuring them that their daily prayers for his salvation would not be unanswered and we agreed to wait on the Lord.

14c   More answered prayers

Four years after my children's dad left us, he had a stroke, so there was no more child support and I prepared to look for a job. My applications had no replies for two months and coming home from another interview one day, I asked my Lord why there was no job for me? About an hour later the phone rang and a manly voice said, "this is Campus Crusade for Christ, is this Hannah Casarez?"

When I answered yes, the man continued "are you still looking for a full-time job?" Agreeing yes, he replied, "would you come to Accounting at eight on Monday morning please." Surprised I told my heavenly Father, "Accounting? but You know I am a Medical Assistant." But I registered, and due to a very patient teacher, I knew and adjusted to accounts receivable.

This generous Creator always hears the prayers of His children and answers them as He knows is the very best for them. Only He knows the outcome and if it is good for their future He can reverse any evil plan set against them. Sometimes we could laugh with Him because the answer was so obvious, but we just did not see it at that time.

Often His gentile hand moved something out of the way and guided in a solution that I did not even notice and all I could do was thank Him with all my heart. I had to ask forgiveness so many times for taking His grace for granted and thought about Him and talked with Him only when needed. That is when He convinced me to spend more time with Him in His Word which brought more wisdom and joy.

15

It is such a blessing to be used

A few years later my loving Creator used me at the city's "Pregnancy and Family Center" for 12 years, where women could come once a month and receive the needs for their little ones up to two years old, without cost. While we kept their records, we were allowed to inquire about their spiritual needs also and we did not only save babies from abortion, but quite a few of the parents found Salvation.

This unconditionally loving God also brought His wonderful peace in many situations. One of my clients, a young man and his girlfriend asked me at their second visit if I would please teach them more of the God I had told them about. It was such a blessed time because their amazement and gratefulness for this amazing Creator made it fun to teach them.

She was seven months pregnant, and he had lost his job, so they were living with her parents. I loved their eagerness, they could not learn fast enough and were full of questions about this awesome God. She gave birth to a handsome little boy named Amadeus and asked me if I would please be an aunt to him, to which I gladly agreed. These Bible studies continued till their son was three years old and they moved far away.

There were similar situations like the precious young mother I saw at the bus station with three little ones and two bags of groceries. I was driving home and passed the station on the end of my street when the Holy Spirit influenced me to turn around and give her a ride home. She had the baby and the groceries, so we tied the carrying case in the back seat as well as the three and the six-year-old.

While driving, I introduced myself to her as well as my job as a missionary and was happy that she was open to that. The young mother was on Welfare but did not have a car, so I told her the times I was available to take her for groceries. I was very pleased when she agreed that she would meet with me for Bible studies, and the Lord allowed this for a year till she made up with the children's father and moved away.

15a   There is no end to my Creators faithfulness

When the Lord had called me back to San Bernardino after the ten years of living in San Clemente, I needed a home. I had enjoyed my life and the fellowship while living in a Mobil Home Park and so I was looking for one in the park where my youngest son Bill and his family acquired one. One of the times I slept at their home because the parents had to be out of town for two days.

The kids and I took an early morning walk. Passing one of the homes, we stopped and admired it. I was especially impressed with the big landscaped front yard, and it had a fireplace, which is something I had loved and prayed for. Well, we continued our walk and as coming home, I called my son and told him about this home I had fallen in love with.

Enjoying our morning walks, the kids and I took another one the following day and passed the same home as the day before. To my overwhelming joy the front of the home had a big FOR SALE sign on both sides of the front. Taking a deep breath, I walked to the front door and rang the bell. The owner answered and I shared with him and his wife my desire to purchase a home in this park.

They were delighted, especially when telling them that I was on staff with Campus Crusade for Christ, which had a great reputation in this big city. We sat down together and figured out the paperwork and future payments. Since I had a big down payment from selling my past home, the escrow took only two weeks, and I moved in. Everyone in the family celebrated with me and thanked our generous God.

I was so delighted that this home was very close to my position, my church and the ministries the Lord had started me in. Since I had attended my church eighteen years before I followed my job with Campus Crusade to San Clemente, it was like coming back home. I joined the youth program AWANA again and help teach the Jr high on Sunday night and the Highschool group on Monday night.

16

The unconditional love of God

After moving back to San Bernardino, I got a phone call from a director I had known previously, asking me to come and work with him. I joyfully agreed because now I was back with my beloved Jesus Film. However, when my director retired, the department was closed so I was praying for a new position with CRU. Two months later the Lord got me accepted with the CRU Highschool Ministry which was exactly what I wanted.

It gives me more time now, on the weekends, to work on my 8th book. It is so amazing to me; the Holy Spirit reminds me of the subjects' people would be encouraged by. As there have been sixty-three trips overseas, to twenty-seven countries, I will tell of one more trip, this one was at a different village in India again. This time I was sent to interview a special story for our Jesus Film Paper and bring pictures.

Here was a pastor who was trying to start another church in that area and had already started five, asking Campus Crusade in Delhi for help with the equipment. The pastor had set up to start the film when a group of soldiers on horses entered his property and stopped the show.

When the man of God said he would not stop his services or the film shows, the terrorists beat him and left. About a week later the same invader came back to the pastor with about half his soldiers and dismounted. The pastor expected just about anything and sent up a prayer for help.

The leader of the group came up to him and apologized for having treated him so badly and asked him if he would teach him and his men more about this Jesus. The man of God happily agreed and now, years later this leader, under the pastors teaching, has also started a church and his men attend faithfully. We praise God and thank Him for all the change of hearts He has brought about.

17

This knowledge growth deeper with time

Our teams, through God's faithfulness become more and more bold seeing their Lord is always in control of any situation and would overrule the enemy's interfering. These precious revelations of our mighty Creator's presence are so valuable to the children He loves. It keeps us going no matter what the enemy throws our way, and it will bring about the final victory.

For much of my Christian life I wondered how I am in Jesus, when in 1ˢᵗ Corinthians 1:30 it said very clearly, "But of Him (the Father) you are in Christ Jesus, who became for us wisdom from God – and righteousness and sanctification and redemption. Therefore, as it is written, "he who glories, let him glory in the Lord." This is perfect, I don't have to ask or wonder anymore, *the Father said so, that's good enough for me.*

It explains in 1ˢᵗ Corinthians 15:21 and 22, "For since by man came death, by Man also came the resurrection of the dead. For as in Adam all die, even so in Christ all shall be made alive." It is so awesome to claim and live by these powerful promises and rely on Him being the same always. That assurance is priceless and no one in heaven or earth can make these promises except our merciful Creator.

My temperature raises high when people question or reject the word of God as truth, because they have not even checked it out or been willing to obey it. Having had the joy of blessings when I obeyed, helps me listen to Him closer than ever. Sharing often, that hearing His voice comes from being in His word as often as possible, that is where our Savior reveals Himself.

He also continues to assure us that His love for us continues to deepen and never ends giving us endless chances to return to Him, should we leave Him at any time. I truly wish I had that kind of patience and love if someone walks away from me leaving much hurt behind. Our Savior says He enables us to remember the love and forgiveness we received when we were unfaithful and deserted Him at any time.

18

God's word stands forever

I share with my students often about that lifesaving word He has written to the children He loves so much. As it says so clearly in 2 Peter 1:20 – 21, "knowing this first, that no prophesy of Scripture is of any private interpretation, for prophesy never came by the will of man, but holy men of God spoke as they were instructed by the Holy Spirit." Since this is all given by God, how would I ever dare question this holy writing.

Many of the Jesus film showings had interruptions from opposing spirits, but prayer was always the answer. Our teams had learned that the interferences came to the equipment, so they were always ready to lay hands on it and pray. I will never forget one of the shows, we had a similar experience the night before, so we took an extra machine.

Sure enough, there was some unrest and as before, the first projector . We set up the second one, laying hands on it quickly and each of us saying a prayer and this time it began to run and never stop. This was very successful and proved once again that prayer is always powerful and gets answered at the right time.

Being welcomed by two elderly men, we set up our equipment, while many children with excitement surrounded our team. The projector ran smoothly, when at the first time Jesus appeared in the film, suddenly, hearing a loud scream, the film screen tore in half. The film team quickly gathered for prayer and put up a new one, while one of the viewers ran out of the audience with loud, violent screams. We were told that this was the village sorcerer.

This was not unusual for our film teams, so, with a new screen the showing was continued. From what could be seen, the entire village received Jesus Christ as Savior. Two of the national Christians on staff with CRU had already volunteered to set up Bible studies. This was pre-planned by our superiors, so that these new believers would not be left without follow-up in learning about this loving and forgiving God. Our film screens were made of parachute material so it was see-through, and we could place our large audiences on both sides of the screen.

19

Such a valuable gift to us

This film, so blessed by God, has been shown in every country in the world since it's completion. It was produced by Campus Crusade for Christ entirely by the Gospel of Luke and filmed for us by Warner Brothers entirely in Israel. We have it by 2023 in over 2000 languages and the DVDs have the entire 2 hr. film on it in twenty-four languages. Like the Bible, it is the most published and seen film in the world, Hallelujah.

Our staff and I show this life of Jesus Christ whenever possible, inland and overseas, and it has resulted in uncountable salvations. It has given us many chances to share our testimonies even in other countries with an interpreter. I give my beloved Father thanks all the time, trying never to take His goodness for granted. I cannot imagine how many times He tells the enemy no, when he tries to harm us.

Another blessed ministry the Lord is using me for where I represent CRU is called "Global Media Outreach". I can participate in the evenings by calling them and they provide me with e-mail addresses of people that have prayed at Christian conferences and received Jesus Christ as their Savior. They now ask what to do next and I can tell them how and where they can find the answers to their questions.

I give them first Colossians 1:13 & 14, which says "God has delivered us from the power of darkness and transferred us into the kingdom of the Son of His love, in Whom we have redemption through His blood, the forgiveness of sins." After a few more scriptures I can help them find a church in their area or one of our Bible study groups. This is a powerful ministry, and we can reach as many as our Lord has planned.

This is a very blessed ministry, and these emails can be answered any time of the day. In the first two years I was able to answer 271 emails and it was a great blessing because these calls could be carried out as far as the people allowed it. It was so blessed to be used by my Savior for this ministry because I could do it at home after work.

19a Having to use "tough love"

One of the lessons I learned from my Bible teacher was hard to follow. When my daughters were on their own and had money problems, my mom and I jumped in to help. That problem happened more often, and I could see they were not wise with their funds. So, I counseled with my favorite teacher, my pastor also having just given a message on this subject. The advice from both were to use tough love.

The answers from both were that we are not helping but harming them. The Lord probably wanted to teach them responsibility and we were hindering that lesson. My stopping the help caused exactly what my teachers said, they got angry with me. My mom would not listen to my reasoning so she lost her job and could not help either.

The good news is that both my girls found jobs in walking distance, and both agreed with my purpose for stopping the giving. They saw that God loved them and always has the best plan. My mom soon got a good job also and everything was in good standing again.

My favorite teacher has always been Chuck Swindoll, I listened to his messages every morning and recorded them as well. He taught only from the Bible, and I could not get enough. Chuck taught that my life is 10% of what happens to me and 90% of how I respond to it. His teachings and books have been a blessing to my oldest daughter and my oldest son as well.

My daughters were married soon, and their husbands had received Christ as Savior and together they were baptized. I was very happy knowing that their children (my grandchildren) would be growing up in the knowledge of the Lord.

20

That precious blood of the Savior

It is so wonderful to trust in and live for my Lord and Savior. It has been so awesome these last forty-eight years. I could never have imagined the joy and pleasure to be in His presence every moment of this earthly life. But this is not all, the very best is yet to come. It helps me, especially in hard times, to dwell on what my future holds for me.

My God has allowed me to come to Him without my baggage, that was all left behind when I gave Him my life. This made it possible to keep running this race, which was laid before me, as long as I kept my eyes on the One who called me. Taking my future seriously and reaching forward, kept my heart and mind on His lifesaving word, believing His powerful promises and warnings.

When I have submitted myself to His will and guidance in the beginning, according to Romans 1 and 2, saying "I beseech you therefore brethren, by the mercies of God, that you present your bodies a living sacrifice, holy, acceptable to God, which is your reasonable service." I could have never imagined the blessed life it would become.

It is wonderful to know that Someone who created such a beautiful world would love and protect me, helping me not to live in fear of my enemy. Jesus Christ defeated Satan with His death and by His blood. It has been such a joy to help my students understand this awesome promise from their wonderful Savior.

Even when Satan asks my Lord to harm me, and He allows it, this beloved Savior prays for me, as He did for Peter. As Peter, I am asked that when I have gone through it, to strengthen the believers around me. Who could ever deny or refuse such a loving and merciful Creator, who patiently waits for His believers to respond to His calling and assurance of love.

For all the hurts and rejections in our past, this Lord has made up for with His deep incomprehensible love and forgiveness. His powerful letter to His children has saved and changed more lives than can ever be counted by us, only by Him. In Psalm 19 it talks so beautifully about our God, especially how it starts out in verse :1, "The heavens declare the glory of God, the firmament shows His handiwork."

21

All about our awesome God

The entire Psalm 19 declares the Glory of this Creator, one of my favorites is verse :7 which continues "The law of the Lord is perfect, converting the soul, the testimony of the Lord is sure, making wise the simple." It just keeps on telling how indescribably this God is, ending in verse 14 "Let the words of my mouth and the meditation of my heart be acceptable in Your sight, O Lord, my strength and my Redeemer."

I believe that is one reason the Lord called David "a man after His own heart." One reason was that David truly repented when he failed, the other was that he so beautifully described his Creator in his Psalms. This is how we learned much about God and how He feels about us.

However, much we learned from the Savior Himself, especially in His prayer to His Father in John 17:20 saying "I do not pray for these alone, but also for those who will believe in Me through their word." Praise God, that includes me by my asking Him to enter my heart and my life and make me what He wants me to be.

This is why it is so valuable to be in His precious word whenever possible because that is where He reveals Himself to us. However, this awesome God has also shown His wonderful imagination in everything He has brought about since day one. Everything that has been created and built has been because He gave humans the wisdom and insights and the materials to complete it as He imagined and planned it.

Jesus also asked the Father in John 17: 23, "I in them and You in Me, that they may be made perfect in one and that the world may know that You have sent Me, and I have loved them as You have loved Me." This totally explains our condition and state we have in our Savior, and He finishes in verse 26 saying, "And I have declared to them Your name, and I will declare it, that the love with which You loved Me may be in them, and I in them."

21 b   To not serve Him half-way.

My beloved Savior deserves for me to serve Him with all my heart because He gave me His all. It means to go forward and not be afraid, because He has shown me His awesome faithfulness and love. One of the many promises that comes from my praising my awesome God is in Psalms 18:3 saying, "I will call upon you Lord, you are worthy to be praised, so shall I be saved from my enemies."

I have learned that praising this mighty God brings Him great joy, that is why Psalms are the best to use for this. For instance, this is a great one, 18:1 &2 "I will love you O Lord my strength. Lord you are my rock and my fortress and my deliverer, my God, my strength in whom I will trust, my shield and the horn of my salvation, my stronghold."

In the mornings I especially love the Psalms, they are written by David and are the best to praise this merciful and loving God. I love it best when I use it in a personal way, like talking directly to Him. I love to make Psalm 23 personal like this, "Oh Lord, you are my Shepherd, I shall not want, you make me lie down in green pastures, You lead me beside the still waters."

Doing this, especially with the Psalms, it makes feel like I am in a conversation with my beloved God and not just talking about Him. My Lord explains John 16:33, "These things I have spoken to you, that in Me you may have peace. In the world you will have tribulation, but be of good cheer, I have overcome the world."

This shows that He has absolutely taken care of everything to make sure His children can live this Christian life. At these times I just love Him for His constant care for me and the ones I pray for. I can walk the world on both sides now, the saved part and the unsaved. That is why it is so important that I cling to the Savior I love, because He never separates Himself from me.

22

And He did plan it all.

Jesus promised in Acts 1:8, that His believers shall receive power when the Holy Spirit has come upon them, and they shall be witnesses to Him. This has been my desire ever since I came to know Him through Campus Crusade for Christ in 1974. This was when my Lord began to teach me and use me. I began to fall in love with this awesome Maker of heaven and earth and all His believers.

One of the many titles our awesome God has is indescribable which means that no one can truly describe the power, greatness, mercy and unconditional love of this mighty Creator. It was at my re-birth that the Holy Spirit entered my life and the first witness I became was to my four children.

Longing for them to begin to know this God of love, I made sure to tell them only the absolute truth from His word, the Bible. This soon became my favorite pastime as I felt the joy of others finding this blessed Savior as I had. This has been since 1974, and I cannot imagine a greater reward than this, even if it means no rewards in heaven.

Not being home with Him yet can only be endured by taking more lost ones away from the enemy. Only in the arms of their Savior can they experience life as He had originally planned it to be. Even though living in heaven has been delayed by Adam and Eve, we will have it all when we are finally home. It will all have been worth waiting for and the best part is that it will never end.

One scripture I have often used and enjoyed is Jabez prayer in 1ˢᵗ Chronicles 4:10 which says "And Jabez called on the God of Israel saying 'Oh, that You would bless me indeed, and enlarge my territory, that your hand would be with me, and that You would keep me from evil, that I would not cause pain." So, God granted him what he requested, and I knew He would answer me also.

23

Answered prayer

The most important part of this prayer to me was that He would enlarge my territory, because I wanted to have more ministry chances. My Lord answered this prayer by arranging for me to represent Campus Crusade for Christ at the city schools. It started out with one Jr-high school for two years, and then added three more high-schools.

The first one was after classes ended, from 3:00 to 5:00, for a program called CAPS and was for students whose parents worked, so the youth had extended school time. I was allowed 15 per room and it often extended for personal one on one prayer requests. There was plenty of time for this because my Juvenile Hall Bible times did not interfere with these.

As I already shared, my time was so free because my children were on their own by now, so these ministries eased my loneliness. The girls were married, and the boys had joined the Service, so the Lord had given me hundreds more children. In near future I learned from Hebrews 6:11 and 12 that it is desired of me to show the same diligence to the full assurance of hope until the end.

It continues that I should not become sluggish but imitate those who through faith and patience inherit the promises. This told me that if I wanted to possess these awesome promises of my heavenly Father, I must continue in imitating and learning from teachers like Paul. Well, the only way I can imitate these blessed brothers of mine is by keeping on studying their lives and messages.

This is what I intended to do and asked the Holy Spirit for His help as it was promised in God's word saying that He will instruct me and guide me. Since He never lies, I decided to live in that wonderful peace He said would be given to me. It began to show me that by not worrying or living in fear, He was able to use that time in my concentrating on Him and helping others in finding that same peace.

24

His promises must be taken seriously

Our God is a gracious God, always covering pain and disappointments with His never-ending love, He promises in John 10:10 that He came to give us an abundant life. What I love and teach the most is John 10:27-30, "My sheep hear My voice, I know them, and they follow Me. And I give them eternal life and they shall never perish, neither shall anyone snatch them out of My hand.

The Father who has given them to Me, is greater than all, and no one is able to snatch them out of My Fathers hand. I and My Father are one." The Bible tells us several times that our God never lies, so this is a never-ending fact to me to pass this on to others seeking Him. Especially the youths at the Youth Detention Center cling to His promise that they shall never perish, when I explain to them that perish means to die in a violent way.

Since it says that we can hear His voice and follow Him, that should make it easy for us to obey His requests. However, we are not perfect yet so the best way to live by our Saviors guidance is by spending much time in His love letter to us. He promises in Psalm 32:8 "I will instruct you and each you in the way you should go, I will guide you with my eye." That leaves us pretty much without an excuse why we do not hear His voice.

These verses also inform us that He says He knows us. So, we can be assured that in everything we are and do, He is already familiar with, so there is no pretending. However, it also shows us how deep His love for us is because He died for our forgiveness in the most crucial way. Our beloved Savior also shows that our sins are forgiven, past present and future, so all we are accountable to Him for is if we lived this Christian live by loving one another.

Loving each other is shown to be the most important thing to the Creator because that is what He mentions most in the Old and New Testament. The only way I can learn to do this is by learning from and imitating these precious men and women before me who lived and followed the word of their God.

25

His presence can be so near

Having had pain in my right hip for a while, one day I bent over and could not straighten back up. My mom took me to the doctor who had me immediately admitted to the hospital. He said kindly that the Ex-ray showed my hip socket being deteriorated and needed to be replaced.

My mom dropped me at the hospital and went home to be there for the boys and encourage my recuperation. After being checked in and taken to a room, I noticed a lady in the second bed. Being scheduled for surgery the next day, neither of us were being served dinner so it was a good time for introduction.

Sharing with my roommate Lucy that I had no fear of tomorrows operation because I knew that God was a total part of it, got her attention. Lucy said she was here because of an accident and was hoping to walk again. I prayed that her hope would be fulfilled, and we both fell asleep due to the medicine given us.

Waking up, my doctor commented that the surgery was successful and wished a quick recovery. When Lucy and I were fully awake she shared with me the trouble she was having with her kids and asked if I would pray for that. Having done that, I told her about having been in the same situation with my teenage daughters.

Only my continued prayer and trust in God's promise of Isaiah 55:11 saying, "So shall My word be that goes forth from My mouth, it shall not return to Me void, but it shall accomplish what I please, and it shall prosper in the thing for which I sent it." Knowing that He sent His word for Salvation, kept my heart trusting Him, staying quiet.

25a   The Lord's promises are so valid.

It was a victory for Jesus to see Lucy smile and commit to trusting her Lord more than she had been. Reaching for my Bible I found some scriptures just right for her need. They confirmed that only her Creator can bring healing to what had been changed by human attitudes.

When He says in Psalm 103:14," For He knows our frame, He remembers that we are dust" is not a put down but that he knows our weaknesses. This shows is great compassionHim being so compassionate when we miss His guidance. Our Savior promises us in Psalm 32:8, "I will instruct you and teach you in the way you should go, I will guide you with My eye."

This scripture I used most of all, especially while needing hope in raising my children. Sharing this also with my roommate Lucy showed her being more relaxed. It convinced her to spend daily time with her Savior in His lifesaving Word. We agreed to meet for Bible study when our lives would allow.

Realizing for the first time that the women the Lord had brought into my life were somehow separated from their husband and had trouble with their children. This was not because I was a good example of a long-lasting marriage, but their child relationships had also been mine before God entered our lives.

Sharing the faithful work our Creator did with my children and me, in spite of my mistakes, showed me why He could use even me. He wanted me to encourage women who are in trouble and hurting, with the same comfort and love He had used on me.

25b   The example of ten virgins

There is no way that I can take credit for anything my Lord has done, I am still only his child, waiting for Him to restore me and fill me as His vessel. Being the clay on His potter's wheel, I must hold still, being formed, and shaped into what He wanted me to be since He first knew me. Again, all the glory goes to My Savior while I trust Him to lead my future.

Another scripture I like to teach, even though it gives me chills is Matthew 25:1-4, where it tells us about ten virgins who went out to meet the bridegroom. Five of them were wise and took oil with their lamps but five were foolish and did not store oil. The oil is usually represented by the Holy Spirit, so I suppose five were using their time to have worldly fun.

Since the bridegroom was delayed, they all fell asleep, however when the call went out that the groom was arriving, the foolish virgins went to find oil. When they came back the door had been shut and the virgins knocked to come in and said, "Lord open to us." However, He answered and said "Assuredly, I say to you, I do not know you."

Ever since then, I asked seriously for the baptism of the Holy Spirit and one church service I went forward and received it. What a blessing to have now a way for more knowledge and understanding of my God's awesome will. Since He lives in me, I do not have to always plead for his coming, because His presence never leaves me. It has been great having this Comforter giving me understanding while I was writing the Bible studies for my youths.

26

The awesome blessing of prayer

A great joy in my life was being baptized in the Holy Spirit and I received the feeling of a greater awareness of my Lords presence. Even though I received some of that precious Spirit when I first received Jesus as my Savior, I wanted all He had for me. When I tried to share this with my family, they were not ready to accept this and so, as I did with their Salvation, I began to pray that they would also receive that gift.

It is sad that even some believers do not experience the wonderful power of the Holy Spirit. Even when this almighty loving Father answers their prayers, I hear them findinge says 'yoyu other excuses for the miracle. This is the only time I would use some of those powerful verses to tell them where their attitudes are leading them and all they are missing of God's blessings.

Praying is the way to communicate with this gracious Lord and get attention to our requests because He says, "you have not because you ask not." Before each of my sixty-three overseas trips, much prayer and awareness preceded. I would not have considered this if there had been fear. So many things could have gone wrong without my heavenly Father's approval.

Only once were we denied entrance into a country however since we gathered and prayed, our God arranged the open door. We could always depend on His answers especially if there was a "no". Prayer always brought the plan Our God had for every situation.

Our obedience also brought blessing and joy, so we were ready for the next project, with even more ideas for witnessing. It says so well in 2nd

Corinthians 1: 21 and 22 "Now He who establishes us with you in Christ and has anointed us is God, who also has sealed us and given us the Spirit in our hearts as a guarantee." I said that about twenty times, with such joy, never to forget it.

26.a God's will always have the victory

There have been unbelievable times and ways of interferences during the film showings, yet no matter what kind of trouble the enemy caused, the Jesus Film was shown. I remember one time, in the middle of the film the sound went out, yet no one left, they all stayed to the end. An unbelievable number of salvations were reported and most of these wanted to lea rn more about this Jesus and His Father.

The One who had prepared all the fixing and repairs was the One who died, so all nations could hear and see the Good News. This gave us the courage to carry on knowing that our God could never be held back or be defeated. We have learned through all this what it says in John 6:63, "It is the Spirit who gives life, the flesh profits nothing. The words we speak to you are spirit and they are life."

When I turned eighty-five and was not allowed to travel overseas anymore, I took a deep breath and did not let disappointment ruin my days. That was because I believed that my heavenly Father had something else once again for me and I waited. Surely it came, and it was to tell those after me how much their God can be trusted. So, he had me take some of my notes from past quiet times and make them into books.

A very powerful scripture my eyes fell on was Habakkuk 2: 2 which told me "Write the vision and make it plain on tablets, that he may run who reads it." To my great amazement it continued in verse :3, "For the vision is yet for an appointed time, but at the end it will speak, and it will not lie. Though it tarries, wait for it, because it will surely come, it will not tarry." Whew, I had to read this several times to take it all in.

So, I continued to write what my Lord brought to my mind, believing with all my heart that the best is yet to come. Knowing from the scripture above to wait for it, because it will surely come. All my Christian life I have loved Revelation. Especially the last two chapters and most of all, because it promises in 22:7," Behold I am coming quickly, blessed is he who keeps the words of the prophecy of this book.

To keep the prophecy of this book I had to read the part of the Seven Churches, and some was scary, but more was a blessing. It depended on how seriously I wanted to be blessed by keeping this word.

27

Believe on Him who justifies

Satan used to make me think because I was so involved in ministries that I was worthy of God's love. Well, thanks be to the Holy Spirit showing me in Romans 4:5 differently by saying "But to him who does not work but believes on Him who justifies the ungodly, his faith is counted for righteousness." It never says that I am worthy.

This was such a relieve to know that my business will not count for me, but of great importance is my faith in my awesome God. Nothing is more precious to my loving Creator than my trusting in all those wonderful promises and just enjoying Him and His word. And enjoying Him has always been my greatest goal because growing up I was always being made afraid of God.

The biggest thing that has changed was spending more and more time in His word. Nothing else is that beneficial. It happened very seldom that my God seemed far away, however when it came about, I remembered that beautiful promise He gives in Jeremiah 29:13 where it says, "You will seek Me and find Me when you seek Me with all your heart." So, as soon as it comes to my mind, I run for the life-giving word of God and get filled again.

It is so important in my having offered to be a "mentor" to several of our girls in the "Joy Company." This is a ministry to city schools where a pastor, his wife and I meet with about thirty high school age youth who want to learn being leaders in their school and future jobs. These youths are serious in wanting to be good examples to their younger siblings and *friends that this Christian life is possible with a close relationship with this almighty loving Creator.*

We also teach the word of God in the city schools and encourage students to join us in other activities we have. This is why it is so important that those who teach them are very familiar with the word of God, to teach only the truth. It is a true joy to see their wanting to learn and use this powerful, life changing letter their Lord wrote to the children He loves so much.

27a   Is teaching your desire?

It says in James 3:1 that we who teach will be judged with greater strictness, so it is vital that we study His word much. It is such a joy to keep the scriptures alive in my mind and add to them as God's word is studied daily. There is no being finished and knowing it all, our Creator never tires revealing His precious word to His children.

Wanting so badly to leave a legacy to those being young now and those coming after, it is like fulfilling a dream by leaving these books for them. My beloved God can use them however He pleases, and I get such a blessing out of the way He gives me the right words to say.

Often the Holy Spirit brings things to my remembrance and has me recall scriptures as authority for them. The Bible says so often to share with others what I have been taught, I try to remember that always, this is where my joy and peace come from. That is what I am called for besides delighting myself in my God so He will give me the desires of His heart and not of my heart.

Having always longed to leave a legacy for my family about the saved part of my life, my Lord moved me to write some special parts of it into books. It seems to me like a command when it says in Habakkuk 2:2 to write the vision on tablets and make it clear that he can run who reads it. I feel that this is what my Father is saying to me.

This is great because now others can read about the great love and protection of this awesome Creator. I have always longed to leave a legacy and a video, now DVD, for my children in case the Lord takes me home before the rapture. Well, it looks like my Savior had something more extensive in mind and I am amazed.

28

Until the blessed calling

It is the blessed Holy Spirit who brings happenings I have forgotten to my memory, and I love reliving them. Never having imagined what a Christian life could be, I am sad to see all the joy and peace I missed out on earlier, but it is truly better late than never. So, I just simply enjoy what I am getting and learning now, being grateful for not having missed more.

This awesome Creator drew me to Himself at the lowest part of my life and showed me that beautiful hope He offers all who believe in Him and His lifegiving son Jesus. I realized that taking my life would never have been a blessing to my four children and so I am glad I waited till I was called and clung to my Savior instead.

Of the tens of thousands my beloved Father has brought into my life, I will never know how many truly gave their life to this loving and merciful God, only He does. However, it was a wonderful journey and what I remember most was His great protection. Experiencing it most in the many places overseas, I had been informed of the danger, yet there was only the blessing of Salvations.

After a while of experiencing that wonderful protection, fear hardly ever came to the surface but grew into a beautiful trust. It has been such a joy to watch all those precious students the Lord entrusted to me, as they began to believe that this big and mighty God could really love them.

Little by little they began to realize that things were going better since they gave their lives to the One who died for them. Hardly any of them had good grades, even my great grandchildren did not, but after they gave their lives to this Savior, not only did their grades greatly improve but the relationship with the teachers did also

29

I keep my eye on the finish line

It makes such a difference when my mind is on the future and the beautiful ending, it keeps my spirit up no matter what the news says. Hebrews 12:1 & 2 encourages us to lay aside the sin which so easily ensnares us and let us run with endurance the race that is set before us. We need to look to Jesus, the author and finisher of our faith, Who, for the joy that was set before Him endured the cross.

This precious Savior, despising the shame, has set down at the right hand of the throne of God. In the meantime, my Lord encourages me with Isaiah 46:4 "Even to your old age, I am He, and even to gray hairs I will carry you." That is so awesome to me, at the age of 85, that He is willing to carry me, how can I give up with promises like these.

Truly I can vouch for His honesty and faithfulness by now and encourage others as I have been encouraged. This is part of the daily prayer for all I care about that He would reveal Himself to them as He has done for me. Falling in love with this wise and caring God will make their lives one of peace and joy being able to love others as He desires for them to.

There is no reason to be discouraged even in hard times because He says in Romans 8:26 and :27 it is promised that the Holy Spirit helps us in our weaknesses. It tells us that because we don't know how to pray, this beloved Spirit Himself makes intercession for us according to the will of God. Our loving Father has truly done everything possible for His children to live this Christian life, even giving up His beloved son.

But to top it all off, He tells us in Luke 10: 19 that He gives us authority over all the power of the enemy and says in verse :20 do not rejoice because the spirits are subject to you but rather rejoice that your names are written in heaven. This is why I try hard to never complain or gripe when things do not go my way or happen fast enough. His will is always the very best, so it needs to be discovered.

30

Make your requests out loud

Having learned that His timing is always perfect, makes it easier to be patient, even though I still have a way to go yet in this. Just having listened to one of my favorite teachers I was made aware of something I agree with. He was teaching me to speak out loud about something I want to happen and wanted to hear the scriptures he used for this.

The first one was Mark 11:23-24 "For assuredly, I say to you, whoever says to this mountain, 'Be removed and cast into the sea' and does not doubt in his heart but believes that those things he says will be done, he will have whatever he says." The other scripture the teacher used was James 4:11, "Do not speak evil of one another, brethren. He who speaks evil of a brother and judges his brother speaks evil of the law and judges the law."

These verses and so many more, have to do with speaking, saying the request out loud, as the prophets used to when they wanted something to happen, and it came about. When I speak with my Creator, I do it mostly in my mind, unless when I am passionate about the subject. For instant, I have a dear friend and when we are together, we talk much about subjects which the Bible speaks strong about, and we agree with it.

What came to my mind was that our God put sinews and flesh as well as skin on a whole army of dead bones in Ezekiel 37 from chapter one to the end. They came to life and were able to fight again which brought glory to our God. This gave me an idea for prayer to my beloved Lord, He loves it when we remind Him of what He said.

31

Seek and you will find

With my beloved Father, answering prayers is His greatest joy and achievement. He loves rewarding those who seek Him wholeheartedly because He promised that He will be found. Our Savior says so beautifully in John 14:12, "Most assuredly I say to you, he who believes in Me, the works that I do he will do also, and greater works than these he will do, because I go to My Father."

"And whatever you ask in My name, that I will do, that the Father may be glorified in the Son. If you ask anything in My name, I will do it." WOW, how could I possibly not trust Him with all my life, what human beings would be able to promise even any part of this. This great and mighty God has kept His thousands of promises to His children, never forsaking any of them.

To my great joy I was able to experience His faithfulness in my dozens of trips overseas to twenty-seven countries without any hurt or problems. The few difficulties thrown our way by the enemy were taken care of by praying and trusting. One of them was by denial of entry into a country and one of them by being held back by security at the border-patrol.

Each time our prayers brought someone an hour or two later to let us in and once even brought us to our quarters. One time I caught Ameba on the way home from India, and calling my doctor she told my daughter to bring me immediately from the airport for an antidote. The next morning my doctor had me come in because my blood sugar level was 645, the normal being only 100 blood sugar level.

YOU SEE! THERE IS A GOD

Not having any idea that I have diabetes I would never have known without my doctor haven given me a blood test, which she usually does not do for Ameba. No one in my family has ever been diabetic, and I have learned that when my sugar is high, I feel great. There are only problems when the sugar level is low and mine is always high.

32

There is nothing more precious than time in God's word

Of the 86 years of my life I have lived only 48 of them with my gracious, indescribable Creator of heaven and earth. I can never imagine why this God of love chose me as one of His own, but I have all eternity to thank Him for it. It would be impossible for me to tell of the joy and gratefulness about being loved and directed through live by such an awesome loving God.

The ending of John 14:18 says "I will not leave you orphans; I will come to you." I cannot think of a more tender promise than leaving me with such great hope for my future. The presence of this amazing God has always been there since the unbelievable day of my Salvation, and this hope has kept me close to Him. It stayed a reality due to my faithful time in that life giving word.

A very good advice is Proverbs 16:32 "He who is slow to anger is better than the mighty, and he who rules his spirit than the one who takes a city." There are so many scriptures about anger because it is one of our greatest troublemakers, even amongst brethren. The Lord has delivered me from some of it, but sometimes it arises still so fast, even though I have begun to think more before I speak.

It has become a delightful challenge to see how long before I put my foot in my mouth or remember the advice from Proverbs 15:1, "A soft answer turns away wrath, but a harsh word stirs up anger." While raising four children I had to learn this quickly if I did not want to lose them. God had entrusted them to me and held me accountable to Him and He truly did His part in helping me.

I know a man who took Ephesians 4:26 very serious, "be angry and do not sin, do not let the sun go down on your wrath" really helped. He never went to bed at night without making sure he had made up with anyone he had offended. This made his life peaceful, especially with those closest to him.

33

Do not worry about what to say

It says about Jesus in Hebrews 2:18 "Because Jesus Himself suffered when put to the test, He is able to help those being tested." Another scripter warns in Ecclesiastes 7:9, "Do not hasten in your spirit to be angry, for anger rests in the bosom of fools." There are many more verses that speak about anger because the writers of this subject had experience in it.

When I first began to give my testimony, usually without being informed, I got so nervous about what to tell them. That was because the people were Christians much longer than I had been and they would realize my mistakes with scriptures.

But then I found a wonderful verse that kept me at peace, it is Luke 21:14 & 15, which says "Therefore, settle it in your hearts not to mediate beforehand what you will answer, for I give you a mouth and wisdom which your adversaries will not be able to contradict or resist."

WOW, this is the most unbelievable thing I have ever been promised that my Savior will give me a mouth so I will know what to answer someone's questions. I use the New King James Version for my scriptures simply because that is what we use in schools and Youth Prisons.

Our teaching must be the same and agree with what it says in the Bible, and the wording must coincide to show that it is the truth given by the Holy Spirit. Teaching teenagers for close to 45 years has been my greatest joy and blessing and I asked to be able to do this till my Lord takes me home.

34

Not the end for witnessing yet

Of course, after seven years in heaven, I get to come back and do it some more for 1000 years, and that in a perfect and new body that can never be harmed in any way, what a wonderful plan. Only a loving Creator could put this all together before He even made the world and started the action. However, since the very beginning it had all be worked out, even when mankind rebelled, He had a solution.

Our Lord has been for a long time patiently waiting to have His beloved children home with Him. In the meantime, I will try to please Him and serve Him the best I am able. Not having to be concerned anymore of what to say when confronted by anyone, helps me to be at peace about why I believe what the Bible says.

I can calmly and freely present the truth, praying that they will receive the beautiful offer of Salvation. It became a reality to my four children as they began to experience the difference these scriptures made in my life. They were willing to be a part of the Bible studies Donna and I had twice a week, and two more evenings when their boyfriends also joined us.

This was a wonderful time of growth and changes in our lives and one after another of our family gave their live to this faithful God. Once again, He had made some painful situations into hopeful ones. It was fun to begin talking with these young people about the stories in the Bibles and laugh when they mixed up the people in them.

We then would search the Bibles and find out who was right, which helped us to be more familiar with the stories and the content of them. Learning soon became fun and not a competition because we grew in the knowledge of our God. My young people began to see the blessed changes the word of God made in their lives.

35

A trip to the San Diego Zoo

My children and I had longed for a long time to visit the zoo and so, on a Saturday we took the two-hour trip. My daughter Lita asked if she could bring a friend, I agreed and off we went with the car full. It was a beautiful drive, passed an Airforce Base, farms, hills and old California mansions.

We brought a nice picnic to eat before entering so we would not have to buy food inside, I could not have paid to feed six people in the park. It was such a pleasure to admire our God's awesome creations, laughing at some, respecting others. The time went by much too fast, but I wanted to drive home while there was still some daylight.

Having forgotten that I needed gas, we began searching for a station but could not find one open. This was that time when all gas-stations closed at 5pm because of gas shortage and my odometer showed empty by now. Since it was 5:30, we began to pray and by faith headed for home, and my young ones said they could feel God pushing our car.

What concerned me was that most part of our way home was past fields and a few farms and March Airforce Base, but no chance for gas. The needle for the odometer was passed empty since we left San Diego one and a half hours ago. My young ones were singing the only three Christian songs they knew, trying not to show fear.

Entering Riverside, I got off the freeway, figuring it was safer on the city streets when the car stopped. It finally did stop and coasted into the gas station next to us right by a pump. The kids came out of the car yelling "it's open, it's open."

Sure enough, a man came from behind the station, explaining he was working on his own car and forgot to lock up. We told him our dilemma and he began to laugh so hard we all joined in. He said, "this is just like our God." He shared about having had a similar situation, and being a believer, the Lord helped him also. After rejoicing we thanked our loving God for once again taking care of His own and will never forget that blessed trip.

36

Our eternal gratefulness to this Father

It was the same Creator God who brought me to such a beautiful knowledge of Him and His word, though I could never know it all yet. I will have to wait for my new body with a perfect mind, and even then, I will get to learn about Him and from Him for all eternity. What a joyous and awesome future.

I always have some soft Christian music playing while I write, it keeps me in perfect peace. Never thinking I would ever write a book, much less seven, I could so depend on the Holy Spirit bringing to my remembrance things I had long forgotten. Like the kind relationships with my family.

My grandparents, who were both widowed, each had three children making it six. They had four more children together, ending up with 10 kids, being raised strictly but with love. This was what makes everyone surprised that I came to America, but there is a saying which states that love grows wherever it falls.

This was my case, and it made me able to leave my family and go to another country. Last January 2023, I had been in the US 64 years and though I love my new home I was still homesick for my old one. So, with the large family I created here in California, I guess this is where I will finish this life and go to be with my Lord.

From the beginning of Salvation, our Lord had led us to a church that accepted us, it was a kind Bible teaching community church. All our blessed knowledge of this awesome God came from there and from Campus Crusade for Christ. Both believed in the Bible and only taught the truth from there.

37

A promise made and kept

After I was saved, there was one strong desire in my heart and the Lord gave me a powerful verse to support this desire. It was Joshua 24:15 "Choose for yourselves this day whom you will serve. But as for me and my house, we will serve the Lord." Finding a plaque as soon as I could, it found a spot on the wall opposite the front door where everyone entering would see it.

When we moved, each time the front door showed this promise to our God. Before Jesus left the earth to go back home, He made sure that we had another comforter, the Holy Spirit, to lead and guide us. Not being able to imagine what I would have done all these years without that precious comforter and guide; I make sure to keep Him close.

The only way to do that is to spend much time involving Him in things I do and plan but also never missing that daily time in God's word. In John 6:37 Jesus stated that "all that the Father gives Me will come to Me and the one who comes to Me, I will by no means cast out." Verse :38 & :39 "for I came down from heaven, not to do My own will, but the will of Him who sent Me.

This is the will of the Father who sent Me, that of all He has given me I should lose nothing but should raise it up at the last day." It is so hard for me to understand how anyone can refuse to follow a gracious God like this. I did till I was 37 because I knew He existed but never heard of His love. This loving Creator even continues with His promises:

He says in verse :40, "And this is the will of Him who sent Me, that everyone who sees the son and believes in Him may have everlasting life and I will raise him up at the last day." His awesome promises are so wonderful, and they become more real as time passes on and we get to know Him in all His beauty and deep love.

"Amazing grace how sweet the sound that saved a wretch like me" is one of my favorite songs which truly describes the change this faithful God of love brought about. His promises are almost too amazing yet are proven to be always true. But they must be believed and received by His children to become reality in their lives.

38

Still Temptations present

My girls had noticed that something really changed in my life but did not quite trust it to be permanent. I used to make many promises but also had to break some of them. My Lord wanted me to trust Him with their salvations and those of the rest of my family and in-laws I was daily praying for.

However, my loneliness was not fully gone yet. Along with reading my Bible every day, I kept spending some of my time in my romance novels. One day, God clearly impressed on me that replacing time in His word with imaginary love affairs was sad to Him. So, gathering up my novels, I put them into a nearby dumpster, deciding to stop it.

This was not the end of my learning, and I began to see that the teachings of the Bible were valuable because after each there was more wisdom for me. While learning the great love of my Savior, there was also a getting wiser to the tricks of the enemy.

There was a weekend coming up advertising a series of romantic movies, all with my favorite actors. Setting up snacks separately for my kids and me, they were told not to interrupt me except at mealtimes and commercials. The dishes were done early, and it was time for me to get involved in stories other people dreamed up.

To my great shock the TV screen was blank and no matter what I tried, it would not play. Calling my sister and asking if I could come and watch just two of my movies on either of their TVs. Sadly, she said that one of theirs was broken and on the other they would be watching their favorite football series this weekend.

39

I got the message now

My girlfriend was on vacation, so there was not one chance to see even one of my movies. So, I spent a lovely weekend with my kids, we saw a great movie at my church after a good potluck dinner. After church on Sunday, we had a nice lunch at our favorite park with friends.

On Monday morning the kids turned on the TV and not to their surprise nor mine, it turned on right away and played without any adjustment needed. I was laughing out loud, because it was unbelievable to me that this God who loved me would go through this much trouble to improve my life.

He also brought to my mind that He did so much more than this by promising that He is going to prepare a place for us. Then He comes to receive us to Himself that where He is we may be also, that was His promise in John 14:2 and 3. So the message was clear once again from my beloved God and my time in His word increased.

Now there were less times of loneliness while His word began to fill my mind and soon there was no more of that. Donna had been taking us to her church and the boys joined AWANA and I did as well, to teach the high school age youths. The Lord showed me in His word that if He did not do the renewing by the Holy Spirit, it would not be permanent.

This is why Jesus made it so important that His followers took His saying in John 14:6 "I am the way, the truth and the life. No one comes to the Father except through Me" serious This needs to be so important to His believers because so many claim that there are many ways to get to heaven when Jesus was so clear on this subject.

Coming to know my Lord deeper with every fellowship in His blessed Word caused me to trust Him more. Especially with scriptures like Isaiah 46:4 "Even to your old age I am He, and even to gray hair I will carry you." A more generous and loving promise nobody could make me, even if I had a husband, he would not be able to make such a commitment because he would also be growing old.

40

I am still in the works

It has been so awesome to live some days in the presence and healing of this unbelievably loving God who never fails one of His promises. He says so lovingly in Exodus 19:5 "Now therefore, if you will indeed obey My voice and keep My covenant, then you shall be a special treasure to Me above all people, for all the earth is Mine."

How could I possibly ignore such a love comment and not try to obey His voice and keep His covenant with all my heart. Being a treasure to my beloved Lord is such a joy to me and I will try to live by obeying His voice. I do not have to worry about hearing Him because He promises in John 10:27 that His sheep hear His voice, and I am His sheep.

So that leaves it up to that obeying part and that I have learned some and got the blessings from it. My Savior suggests in Psalms 37:4 that I delight myself in the Lord and He will give me the desires of my heart, but I do not pray for that. Asking to give me the desires of "His" heart is much wiser because I do not trust the desires of my heart, they have gotten me into trouble in the past.

Listening and obeying took me a while because my mind was too much on me and what I wanted. After all, my first 37 years were lived without that precious Savior and his mercy and forgiveness. There was so much to be unlearned and turned around, I was not good at understanding nor in forgiving. It took a while before I realized what dying to self even meant.

Not until my Savior came into my life and made something usable out of me and even then, it took some work before I was pliable in His hand. I needed to become something He could shape and mold into a representative of His love. This is something I want with all my heart, but the enemy is still working against it.

41

A new kind of teaching

The beginning of my Bible classes at the city schools was something new and unusual to me. I had twenty to twenty-five students who came to my class by choice. This was an after-school program for Jr high and high school kids whose parents worked, so they got to stay after school and choose whatever program they wanted to participate in.

It was such a joy to me that they freely chose this Bible class and faithfully attended. I love the pictures of my groups and pray for them, some stayed after the class to ask for special prayers. Loving their participation made me choose the subjects carefully, just as I had done the thirty-five years in the Juvenile Prison Center.

Another wonderful chance to work with junior-high and highschoolers was in my many years in the AWANA programs of the two churches I was a member of in Southern California. This is a wonderful Christian Program for churches, with colored teams in sports and scripture memorization.

All these groups receive points and awards which go in their books and as pins onto their uniforms. Every quarter of the year there are award nights where trophies were presented, and my two sons and I participated. It was a great way to keep up with recalling that precious word of God and the activity with my boys.

I especially enjoyed the high-school groups because they took it all more seriously than the younger ones. The high school years were my favorite ones with my own kids as well and I got to know that age group very well and am challenged by them. They always took their future more seriously than the Jr high groups.

42

Relent means to change your mind

At one of my morning Bible teachings someone said that our God never relents, however I recalled at least two incidences. One of them is in the story of Jonah in 3:10, where Jonah was disobedient to God's command to go to Nineveh. Jonah did not want God to save these wicked people and went the opposite direction.

After a very large fish swallowed Jonah and spit him back out, he went to Nineveh to tell the people of God's plan. The whole city was sorry and changed their ways and listened to the warning and became good. It says that God relented and did not destroy them as He had planned.

Another story is in Exodus 32:14 where it tells us that Moses was on the mountain and God told him that He will consume His people. Moses pleaded for the people and asked the Lord not to destroy them and turn from His fierce anger. Then it says in verse :14 "So the Lord relented from the harm which He said He would do to His people."

It was so awesome to me that this God we worship, even when treated so wrong by His people, would still have mercy on them. This amazing Creator, even though having been offended, has so much love as to be forgiving great sinfulness. He has wiped away my sins and will do it for anyone who asks for forgiveness.

That was the reason for taking on a very painful death and have the sins of mankind loaded on Himself. This is the greatest love, and it has never changed since the very beginning and will not change for all eternity. Believing in this greatest love story will make any trouble worthwhile, knowing that the trouble is only temporary.

43

One of my miraculous trips in Jordan

This time I headed for Jordan and as always, I lived with Campus Crusade for Christ staff. It was a wonderful Christian family relationship and I got to enjoy their church family as well. Showing the Jesus Film was their expertise and they had dozens of TVs that were used daily to offer the film and the Gospel in any area willing to view God's gift.

Once again three of our men and I packed up to show this valuable two-hour movie to a group of refugees. These men and their families were from another country waiting for their Jordanian citizenship. The women and children were never allowed to attend any meetings with this nationality, so there were supposed to be about thirty-five men coming after working in the fields.

On our way there, we kept driving lower and lower and it kept getting hotter every moment. I asked my partners if they knew their goal when they explained that it was going to be in the Jordan valley, the lowest place on earth. We then just passed a large bolder with some writing and numbers on it and my buddies said that from here on we were going to be with fish, meaning below sea level.

That did not comfort me, but I was sure that our beloved Savior was in charge and control of this venture. When we reached what seemed to be the bottom of this valley, one of my guys told me to get my passport ready. Shocked I said, "my passport"? We are in Jordan and are showing the film in Jordan, I did not bring my passport."

Now it was their turn to be shocked and they told me that we are showing this precious movie right against the Israeli border and must pass through three border guard stations. They continued to explain that we must provide not only our passports but have to get out of the car while it was thoroughly searched.

44

Once again, prayer was the answer

My partners kept mentioning that our car would be searched for weapons. My partners did not want to leave me there in no-mans-land and I did not want those 35 men miss seeing the Jesus Film, so we prayed with all our hearts as we approached the station.

The three soldiers guarding the checkpoint did not carry their rifles over their shoulders but in their hands, so the guard's weapon was in our driver's face when he looked in. My partners showed total surprise when the guard looked at each of us and waved us to move on, while he stepped back.

My three Christian brothers could not get over what just occurred, they said this never happened before. The very same thing took place at the next two checkpoints, the guards looked at each of us and stepped back to wave us to move on, and we just kept praising our awesome God. At the film showing, instead of the 35 attenders 96 had come, and almost all prayed to ask Jesus to be their Lord and Savior.

After the film show most of them wanted prayer and so the four of us left for home way after midnight. We were singing and thanking our God all the way home. Someone at the film showing revealed to us an easier way home, it would be almost one hour longer, but no more checkpoints to cross.

We gladly took the longer way and sang praise songs to our protective Savior all the way to where we stayed that night. Sharing with everyone our miraculous trip brought praises and applause from all who heard.

However, I was not surprised, I realized that my heavenly Father knew that this old child of His had not brought her passport and so He acted as usual. This was not the first nor would it be the last time. As a matter of fact, the next time was only three trips later, on the way to Ukraine.

45

The lovely Ukraine

Being delighted to help with the Ukraine project I ordered my tickets right away. Having been in the surrounding countries I knew exactly what to pack since it was September once again. Being melancholy because it felt like the old, laid-back country I grew up in, and I had no problem making friends, it seemed all so familiar.

The teachers took on the new program quick and easy and invited us to come to their school classes the next morning. Wanting us to watch them use what we had taught them the day before, it was satisfying for them to hear our praise of having done well. They acted out some of the stories and took the Bible seriously.

On Sunday we had time off and visited a beautiful beach in Yalta. It had large ships and boats anchored and some could be rented as long as one month. There were also two castles which had no entry on Sundays, so we only took pictures of it with our team for remembrance. However, the restaurants were open, so we got to taste some of their delightful dishes.

As in the other countries we were also there to train the teachers and leave the Christian curriculum for them to instruct their students. Once again, the welcome was with bread and salt, the meaning of friendship. The pictures of all these times have brought never to be forgotten memories into our lives and lasting prayers.

In the evenings, as in some other countries, a group of senior women performed some national dances. The men did the music while all of them were clothed in their national costumes and after that the students also danced for us. It was a very emotional evening leaving good impressions, not feeling like we were foreigners. There were each time sad farewells even though it was always just a ten-day visit per city.

46

A most awesome promise

After putting my life in the hands of my Savior, I questioned my belonging truly to Him and being completely forgiven. This was because my knowledge of the scriptures was not complete yet and that is why it was so necessary for me to be in that word of God at least once a day. This is also how I finally became sure and confident in being my heavenly Father's child and my faith grew stronger.

I loved what His word promised me in Ezekiel 36:26 "I will give you a new heart and put a new spirit within you, I will take the heart of stone out of you and give you a heart of flesh." I accept that gladly and will never stop searching for my Father's precious word, receiving wisdom and insight. I cannot believe how I got to where I am today, it had to be totally my Creator's will and purpose and I am so very grateful.

It has been such an amazing and joyful journey, and I would not change one moment of it, even with the trials and tests. They have all brought me to a real and deep relationship with this awesome indescribable Creator, who is far from being done with His children. With the very best yet to come, how could I possibly give up, knowing that fear comes only from the enemy.

My oldest son and youngest daughter had their weddings at the chapel of the Arrowhead Springs Hotel. The reception was in the Roman Room with many memories and pictures. Besides me, five of my family members also worked there so this place is very special to us. Steve had a job there as soon as he came out of the Army as security guard at the front gate.

Most of my training was received at Campus Crusade for Christ and was increased by my daily times in God's lifesaving word. I grew also by the many conferences held there given by well-known speakers and pastors. My job has lasted 47 years so far, and I hope my beloved Lord will take me home while I am in mission work when it is time to go.

44

One more of the mission trips

This one was another one in India and was scheduled knowing there may be some opposition. The road conditions were bad so we could only use their tricycles for our transportation and equipment, and we carried the witnessing materials in our hands. The trees being so old, their roots stuck out of the ground making it impossible to use even the smallest cars.

Suddenly it began to rain hard, and we had to decide. We could not show the film that day, but since we were so close to that village, we would promise them another day. After just 5 more minutes we were at the edge of the village and had a blessed surprise. There was not even one drop of rain, but a clear star filled sky.

It took us a minute of amazement before we realized that our Creator wanted our film shown that night. We were welcomed by the eldest of this village, a very old and friendly lady, and were invited to a tour of the area. We were told that it was a special honor to be invited in, it was a rare privilege which seldom happened.

The people were very proud of their living quarters which were about 6' tall huts, clean and with rock circles for cooking. The women were showing of their children and the ladies kept turning their heads so we could see the jewelry pressed into the right side of their nose. They had already eaten their dinner and were waiting to see the film.

Our four men had unpacked the equipment and we started with prayer done by our interpreter. Earlier that evening I had a chance to tell the children, with help of the interpreter, "Who" this film was about and what this Jesus could do for them. I was able to feel the expectation in the air and was asking my beloved Savior to open their hearts to His message.

48

The usual emotions displayed

Once again, the only electricity available to plug in our projector at night was the village's temple, and as usual we got permission to use that power. So, once again as in past shows, we hung up our large screen which was now surrounded by their idols. Showing our pictures of these presentations to our donors and supporters, who made those shows happen by their giving, brings great joy.

It is such a blessing to watch the audience's feelings as they begin to like Jesus for His kindness and care in this film. Not only because this was probably the first movie they had seen, but it was in their own dialect. It was also about a person they had never heard of, and He had a special gift for them. We also experienced the same heartbreaking weeping when He was crucified, not having done anything wrong.

It was all turned around for them when they laughed and clapped and rejoiced at His resurrection from the dead. I thought maybe our audiences in the US were not this emotional about this movie because they had heard about this Jesus at one time or another. It was a joy to also see the great number that prayed the salvation prayer this night and wanted to hear more about this Jesus.

Our local Campus Crusade staff have always Bible study groups set up for these new believers so they can become churches. This so pleases our beloved Savior and as usual this is not the end of this miracle either. We had taught the young people that "Hallelujah" means "praise God" and I have the picture and the DVD of us leaving and the children following us calling hallelujah-hallelujah while the rain begins to fall all around.

How could I describe the awesome love and gratefulness in my heart for this saving God. He continues to let me experience His unconditional love and mercy, even though I do not deserve it any more than at the very beginning of my walk with him. Deserving has never been the subject, it has always, and will be forever, His deep love for those who believe in Him.

49

His mercies are new every morning

Having had a recent fall, I learned something new to share with you. Returning from my Wednesday night Bible study and closing the patio gate behind me, I fell suddenly very hard on the floor. Realizing that I was not able to use my phone and did not have enough air to yell for help, so I said out loud "Daddy I need help." Suddenly the sliding door of the patio opened, and my daughter and her Australian Shepherd came out.

Seeing me laying there, she kneeled beside me and dialed 911, who came and delivered me to our nearest emergency Hospital. I was immediately taken care of and placed in a room at the nurse's station. The miracle of the whole situation was that my daughter had fallen asleep as she always is when I come home on Wednesday.

Suddenly Her dog started to wine louder than he had ever done and began scratching hard at her bedroom door. She hurried to let him out and so maybe saved my life because I was not able to move or call for help and would have laid there all night with the back of my head soaked in blood. My beloved God will always find a way to help and rescue, even using dogs, many of my friends agreed to that.

The other thing that was so miraculous was that there was never any pain, not from the fracture in the hip nor on the shoulder nor the two-inch cut on the right side of my head. I was not even aware that my head was bleeding until I was in the hospital and two nurses kept washing the blood out of my hair until that two-inch cut was sealed.

With the dozens of mission-trips in this country and overseas, what I appreciated most were His endless times of keeping me safe. Even though the enemy once again wanted me out of his way, I could never have counted all the times of my Savior's protective hands. Though I have developed a greater awareness of His presence with me, that was the only way I could have been witnessing about His wonderful peace even at hard or painful times.

50

His promises are to be claimed

One of the promises to be relied on is Lamentation 3:22 and 23 which says, "Through the Lord's mercies we are not consumed, because His compassions fail not, they are new every morning, great is His faithfulness." I am so grateful for my Creator's thousands of promises which make this Christian life possible because of the great hope which is given by them.

Another one of my very favorite Bible verses is Jeremiah 29:11 which promises, "I know the plans I have for you (your name), declares the Lord, "they are plans for good not evil, to give you a future and a hope." That wonderful hope is life eternal with Him without end, in that place that Jesus promised to be preparing for us right now.

My friends and I have been wanting to know, if it took the Lord only six days to create this awesome world, what must this place which Jesus is preparing for almost 2,000 years be like? I can hardly wait to see Him and all that He is about. I am so amazed at His creation now, even though this is the old stuff, which will be brand-new someday soon.

Not being able to do anything but praise Him now, with my limited knowledge of Him makes me anxious to have my new mind and unlimited wisdom. I long to tell my God how worthy He is of our constant worship, but I do not seem to have enough words. However, when I have my new mind which will be in that new body, I can tell Him forever.

These promises, commands, warnings, and insights can help me solve any problems in my life if I am willing to live by them. My beloved Father has made everything available if I am not too proud to accept it and use it. If I use my own opinion and wisdom I will never succeed in this present life.

51

Passing on the awesome examples of God

Jesus having taught His messages mostly by giving us examples so those of us who believe can catch the meaning. I have been truly challenged by believing the truth in His stories and trying to relate it to my life. One story is the powerful meaning for us in 1st Corinthians 6:19 -20 which reminds us "Or do you not know that your body is the temple of the Holy Spirit who is in you, whom you have from God, and you are not your own. For you were bought with a price, therefore glorify God in your body and spirit, which are God's."

Wow, I began to take that seriously, if that is true, I had to make a few changes. Wanting to improve some things I had to decide which were physical and which were spiritual. On the physical side, maybe I needed to consider healthier dishes and an air-fryer. In the spiritual side, I could improve on being more times in my father's word and giving up one or two of my loved movies Saturday and Sunday.

Well, my Lords protection never stopped and one evening the kids and I went to a nursery to pick up some tomato plants for my garden. Coming to Kendall, I would have to turn left and go up over Little Mountain. Well coming down the mountain was a very long truck with the blinkers showing he was turning right into the street where I was stopped.

Waiting till I could be sure the truck was really turning, I stepped on the gas to make my left turn, when suddenly a car came at great speed out from behind it. Being in the lane I was supposed to turn into, it was about to crash right into us. The car had been totally hidden by the big, extra-long truck but suddenly was pushed to their left, missing us by a few inches.

That car kept right on going, never slowing down, or stopping. Taking a deep breath, we all agreed that only a mighty hand could have moved that car away from us. Being grateful would be a great understatement, we just sat still for a few moments and thanked our protective God once again. Our appetite had shrunk, and we wanted no more tomato plants that day.

52

The Big Panorama fire

Having been home from the hospital with my hip-replacement for three days, I was learning to get around with my walker. About 7am, Billy was coming inside from feeding the boy's rabbits, saying that there was a big fire in the hills north of us. Following Billy and Stephen outside Chris and I were checking out the fire.

My sons were leaving for school by then, Billy was walking distance now and Stephen was being picked up by his school bus. We saw how quickly the fire spread across the top of the mountain range, but no one seemed concerned. We knew most of the neighborhood was at work, so we turned on the TV-news station but no news yet.

At 10am Chris came in from the backyard saying that the fire was beginning to come down toward the homes in the foothills. We were out of milk so Chris used her car to rush to the nearby little market so we could make little Christopher's formula. This time of the year the Santa Anna Winds were strong, and they had just started up.

Suddenly the local helicopter flew over and announced to prepare to evacuate our area and to shut all windows. Chris had hoped to be back before baby Christopher would wake up because I could not pick him up yet. Also, we had to get Billy from school, so as usual, I began to ask our Lord for help.

By now the helicopter came a third time announcing that police personnel were coming to our homes to assure the evacuation from homes.

I did not know where Stephen's Bus would drop him off since the streets were announced to be blocked off.

The boy from across the street had come over, knowing I was still immobile, to tell me that the schools were being evacuated. Also, there would have been no way to get little Christopher and me out of the house in time without Chris. But God was in charge, just then Chris pulled in the driveway and being so sharp, had already picked up Billy.

53

No end to God's miracles

So, once again I called on the Lord for help and Chris agreed with me. It was planned for us to stay at my sisters for now, but the problem was how to find Stephen. Oh, our God was in full control of course and one mother knew where my sister lived. She picked up her son from school and took Stephen with her and dropped him off at my sisters.

In my mind I was giving Jesus a big hug, knowing that this was a gift to me, however the excitement was not over yet. Suddenly Chris announced that she could not just simply stand by and let our home of twenty-one years go up in flames. Our screams of protest were of no use since Chris had already jumped in the car and was pulling out of the driveway.

My mother tried to console me, reminding me that there were police everywhere and the streets were barricaded. However, she did not know our Chris very well, she was too much like me, aggressive and bold. Placing her once again into the hands of the God who loves her was easier this time. Knowing that He would be there with her, made me be still and let Him be God.

About twenty minutes later the call came from Chris, telling us that our house would be next because our neighbor's roof was beginning to smolder from some sparks that had landed on it. Just then we heard the Firemen enter the yard and were yelling at her to get out of there immediately.

Suddenly an overwhelming thought entered my mind about our three pets. In all the hurry to get out and grab at least a few pieces of clothes for the next few days we had forgotten about them. My heart ached over having to tell my kids about the pets. One was my canary called Woodstock and the boy's two rabbits.

54

Our God always takes His word serious

The following morning the Sheriff's informed us that it was safe to return to our house and we were ready in no time. We had to go home the long way because not all the streets were open yet, so we followed instructions. We held our breath as we got near our home because we had no idea what to expect.

Well, the house looked clean and whole as when we left, but our greatest delight was hearing my canary just singing away. Billy came running inside carrying his bunny, saying Stephen's was under the rosebushes, it seemed the firemen freed the bunnies. Our gratefulness to God was endless, our Lord once again proved to be so faithful.

Having our house totally replaced and renovated through our own fire, it would have seemed so wasteful to lose it now through another fire. We had planned to sell the house and move to Colorado so this plan would have to be greatly postponed. So, I informed my boss that this Colorado move would have to take place later.

None of my resumes had been replied to yet so there were no cancelations needed, we just had to deal with our disappointments. However, our wishing had to be continued, and we truly believed that was the future given by our Lord. It was good that we still wanted God's will and not our own, so we just waited for our heavenly Father to show us the next step.

There were other changes and postponements to be made, thanks to God there were no relationships to be altered or to end. However, since the Panorama fire did not destroy our house, the Colorado move was still in place, and we kept waiting for God's go! We believed strongly that He would show us what that plan is and we would obey it.

A few days later we received a letter from the insurance company and opening it we thought it would be about $250.- for having done our own cleanup. Opening the letter I did a double take and called Chris, I could not believe what I saw. The check was for $1,264.00, we had our approval for our trip to Colorado.

55

Colorado or bust

Since my daughter Chris and the baby were supposed to come with us to Colorado there would been no room in my car. To make a long story short the Lord gave me a Ford motorhome which fit us all comfortably, even to sleep everyone well. So, on Easter Sunday morning we loaded everything, including ourselves, into the motorhome and after some prayer time, we took off. Chris had even made a big sign for the back stating in red color, "Colorado or bust,"

We had a wonderful trip to New Mexico and spent our first night there at one of the planted KOA camps. The second day we reached Colorado Springs where my first job interview was scheduled. The second one was planned with the Navigators ministry, so we all went in my motorhome to my first appointment which was with the Nicky Cruz ministry.

My interview was delightful, we just enjoyed each other and looked forward to working together. We stayed two more days in Colorado Springs looking at homes. The only disappointment was that we would not be able to live in the mountains, which is what we were dreaming about. It would have been a two-hour drive to work and the same back home.

We were quite disappointed but all we could do was trust the Lord to show us His plan. After a month and a half, the Nicky Cruz ministry called me and said they could not wait any longer and must hire a person from their area. So, we gathered for prayer and thanked the Lord for His answer and considered that subject closed.

To make another story short, four days later a family came and bought our house for cash. We found a beautiful new A frame in Running Springs and two weeks later our family moved us into our new home in the beautiful San Bernardino mountains. I got to remain with Campus Crusade for Christ, and it all ended up being the right our dream come true. Since our faithful God let us see that Colorado was not what we had hoped for, we would not keep talking and dreaming about the right pace for us.

56

Learning about tithing

Reading the first time about tithing I was amazed, never having heard about it and it brought many questions. So, Donna showed me in the Bible were God said in Malachi 3:8 "Will a man rob God? Yet you have robbed Me in tithes and offerings. You are cursed with a curse for you have robbed Me."

In verse :10 He continues, "Bring all the tithe into the storehouse, that there may be food in My house, and try Me now in this," says the Lord of hosts, "If I will not open for you the windows of heaven and pour out for you such a blessing that there will not be room enough to receive it."

I was totally amazed at such a powerful warning and promise, I was just overwhelmed. But then God continued in verse :11, "And I will rebuke the devourer for your sakes, so that he will not destroy the fruit of your ground, nor shall the vine fail to bear fruit for you in the field," says the Lord of hosts.

This sounded awesome to me, and I realized that the fruit of the ground and the vine meant my paycheck to me. It really impressed me that my Lord would rebuke Satan from destroying what I have left after I pay my tithing. So, I have never missed tithing, I had to read this many times before I could remember it all.

There were a few examples for this to happen, but I will give only two of them because each is different. It was payday but it was not a full check, so my plan was not to tithe this time. My sons and I went grocery shopping and while checking out, we were excitedly talking about a program our church was having that evening.

As we drove out of the parking lot, we realized that none of us had taken the groceries with us. Returning as quickly as we could, we were told that someone had already taken them. Checking out the amount of my receipt, I realized that it was exactly the amount I should have been tithing this month.

57

What you give you get back

There was also a giving example, having been invited to hear a missionary couple at an evening service. They had a great need, and my heart went out to them. All I had in my pocket was a twenty-dollar bill but that was my payment on Monday morning for my electric bill.

I remembered that the Bible said in a few places give and it will be given back to you, but that was not my motive this time. They desperately needed a truck for their overseas mission, and I wanted to help. Satan called me a fool, but I told him to go where he belongs and dropped the bill in the basket.

On Monday morning I volunteered at Campus Crusade for Christ, when one of my coworkers handed me an envelope. She said that the Lord had given her family extra this month and He wanted me to have it. Opening the envelope slowly, I got emotional, and the tears flowed because out came the exact amount of my electric bill

Here is a cute tithing story from one of my children which will always be remembered. As soon as had I heard the lesson of Malachi 3, I immediately taught it to my children. My kids each used to get five dollars allowance a month, that is all I could do on my income then. They and I got so many lessons out of that powerful teaching.

It was Sunday at church that Stephen turned in his tithing of fifty cents, and after the service we went up to the hotel pool. The pool was empty so people must have just left for lunch. We had brought some sandwiches, but Stephen first wanted to jump in the water. He saw something floating in the water and I told him to throw it out because it looked like a crumbled leaf.

Suddenly he began laughing very hard, showing us the crumbled piece from the water. We all realized it was a five-dollar bill and joined him in his laughter. We realized that the Lord had given him back the 10% of what he gave at church this morning, but I had to explain to Stephen and the rest, that this was a great lesson how important tithing is to our God.

However, I told them this is not how He always repays when we obey Him, there are thousands of other ways as I have seen it. Explaining they understood that God does not need their money but awards their obedience. He is not delighted with sacrifices, but He is with the obedience of His beloved children, this is what brings Him joy.

58

Oh the blood of Jesus

The Lord showed me in scriptures that Satan has no more power over me, since Jesus' blood is covering me. There is nothing I can do or add to that perfect sacrifice, and nothing my now powerless enemy can take away from it. The best teaching that helped me was one morning at work when one of my Christian brothers gave his testimony.

Sharing to have the problem with the Devil bringing guilt and how the Savior told him to tell this enemy how Jesus' blood had washed us white as snow. He said to add that it was the reason for our salvation. The Scriptures tell us to bring up that precious blood often because Satan knows that is what defeated him. Jesus tells us in Hebrews 10:14, "For by one offering He has perfected forever those who are being sanctified." Hallelujah!

Taking this seriously gave me peace again and I have brought up that saving blood again whenever the enemy shows his ugly head. This is how we grow and win one victory at a time. I was on my way again and the Holy Spirit showed me that He was there all along. Our next teachings came from a youth project we had been involved in, called AWANA.

I have shared other stories already, but here is one more. Calling her Cinthia and her sister Sarah, two sisters having joined our youth club. Sadly, they always arrived late because of the long way they had to walk. We all got together and found people to pick them up and I could take them back home. The girls were so happy to be able to come and soon they also attended on Sundays.

Well, it was Stephen's wedding day nine years later, and the ceremony was at the Arrowhead Springs chapel and the reception in one of the conference rooms. A young women walked up to my son and asked if he knew a lady with his last name called Hannah. He said that was his mom who would arrive for the wedding when it starts.

She explained that she is the wedding planner for this hotel now, but she was needed somewhere else in an hour. She asked him to please tell me how grateful she and her sister are that I helped them in the AWANA years. She wanted me to know that they both still attend the same church, and she has a job with Campus Crusade now. What a blessed memory for me.

59

Another hip-surgery and the roommates.

This roommate I will name Lucy, she was brought in my room after I had been checked in. Dinner was just being served, so this was a good time for a conversation. After introducing myself I asked her the reason for being here. She continued telling me that this was due to an accident, and it was the second surgery to get her walking again.

My surgery was scheduled for the next morning and hers for the afternoon, so I told Lucy that I had no fear of that time. Sharing with her that this was being my third surgery on the same hip, for the same reason, and that God had been there every moment for my last two. She listened intently till we started to fall asleep, and I asked God for a good night for us.

My heart was at rest regarding home, knowing that Lita and Chris were helping my mom take care of the boys. After my surgery my doctor commented that everything went unusually well, and I should be home in one week. Lucy was just being prepared for her surgery and I had a chance to remind her Who was at her side the whole time.

Lucy came back too late for us to talk that night, so I prayed for our save and restful night. The following morning, I shared Christ with her, and she began to cry, telling me that things were bad in her marriage. After she asked Jesus to be her Lord and Savior, I shared some great scriptures and told her if she let the Holy Spirit use her with her husband, that wonderful things could happen.

Promising her a Bible which my mom brought me that afternoon, I assured her that there was no better help to make things right between her and her husband, now that she belonged to the Savior. There was only one more afternoon for me to assure Lucy that this God of love will never leave her or forsake her. She was smiling when she left to go home, and we promised to stay in touch.

60

Sharing the same comfort I received

Lucy came for a visit to my home about seven days later and with joy I began to share about the changes in the lives of my children and me. Sharing a little about our hurtful past, and how He changed it, she really relaxed because she saw that I could relate to her troubles since I went through my own. I could promise that her Creator would take control of the situation from now on and her marriage would heal.

One of my favorite scriptures I shared with her was Psalms 91:14 which promises, "Because you have set your love on Me, therefore I will deliver you, I will set you on high because you have known My name." What a total blessing and Lucy was impressed as well with the assurance of having finally found Someone to see her through the hard times. And the joys and good changes in our lives gave her hope for theirs.

Lucy came to see me at Christmas and brought her husband and mom and we had a blessed time talking about God's wonderful plans for His believers. She had made me a lovely basket with flowers on top and I gave her a study Bible. On the way out she whispered that things are going better with her marriage, and I hoped to see her soon.

My next roommate in the hospital was a young lady. Getting out of bed was still hard for me but I was hoping to get a wheelchair soon. One morning I kept hearing someone cry across the hall from my room. I begged my nurse if I could not get into a wheelchair, I was doing better with pain. She listened to my plea and as soon as was placed in it I took off for across the hall.

I had asked the nurse who was crying in the room across from me and she said it was a young lady named Nancy. Excusing myself, I got closer and asked if I could do something for her. She answered that the pain medicine was not helping at all, and she wanted something stronger. Asking the nurse, the reply came that it was not quite time yet, so her crying got softer and finally stopped.

61

A God for every situation

My question If I could help her seemed strange to Nancy, seeing the position we were both in. Her bell had fallen to the floor, and we were both unable to pick it up, so we began to laugh which got her nurses attention. Nancy's attitude began to change, and she listened carefully in our Bible studies. I was able to give her a Bible and she promised to read it every day.

Nancy shared with me that she was in a fight in school and fell, injuring her knee and her boyfriend had just broken up with her. She admitted having a bad temper and we asked the Lord for help with that. Well, from there on we met more times in the guest room, both being in our wheelchairs. Nancy accepted Jesus as her Savior and Lord, which she said made her very grateful to Him.

After another therapy and lunch, they put us back in the wheelchairs and Nancy and I headed back to our big window. I had one more day before my release and I wanted to make sure my new little sister in Christ would continue seeking Him. Sharing with Nancy a little of the past in mine and my kid's lives made her more relaxed, seeing that God could be trusted.

This was one of dozens of young women I have met, who come from a broken home. They fall for the first man that speaks about love but when they are deserted, they give up on life. This is also what happened to Nancy, but now she has this hope, and her Savior will get her out of this valley of darkness into His blessed light.

Because this awesome Creator has chosen me and given me a new start in life, He will assuredly do the same for everyone who calls on His lifegiving name. I cannot imagine how, in these insecure days, anyone can experience peace and face their tomorrow without God in their lives. He has never left or forsaken me.

62

My two boy's enlistment

As I expected but tried not to think about, Steve joined the Army and Bill the California Conservation Corps. The pain of my empty nest was great, but my God had already worked on this. Bill has always loved the outdoors, planting, and growing things and while in high school he was a volunteer fireman in our city.

Long before my boys were to leave, I started to ask their heavenly Father to give them Christian roommates. After Steve settled in, He called me to let me know that the his roommate was a believer and the two of them would attend church on Sundays together. You can imagine how happy this mother was.

While Steve was stationed in Colorado, I had a chance to visit him twice a year and got to stay those five days with Campus Crusade staff who lived there. On the weekends this family took him in and shared their home and church with him.

Bill graduated from the same high school as his brother, and his training and first camp were in northern California. He and his partner were to take out the huge trunk of a very old dead tree. He and his partner were working opposites when Bill noticed the name tag of his partner who was his superior.

He said to him, you have the same last name as my married sister. His boss lifted his head and looked at Bill's tag and said you have the same last name as my sister-in-law has. Laughing hard, they realized that they were related by marriage. This began a beautiful friendship with Dave and his family, and I got to meet them too as I visited twice a year. We are all still good friends now.

63

The blessed ministry with my Marines

One of my grandsons, Christina's boy, signed up for the Marines and the family joined at celebrating his graduation in San Diego. Since he was stationed at Camp Pendleton Marine Base, and I worked just 30 minutes away, I visited him three times a week. We would meet on Base, sit in my van, and have snacks and study the Bible. Soon one of his buddies would join us and a few days later another would come. The Holy Spirit inspired me to do this for more young soldiers.

Finding out that it was the Navigators staffing the Bible teachers for the California Bases, made me find out where to start. Making an appointment, I met with the top man who happily gave permission for me to hold Bible studies on Base. The man told me they had a couple there from Campus Crusade, but they were transferred overseas. He mentioned that sadly the only place to hold the studies was in one of the Quonset Huts.

The man warned that these huts were hot in the summer and cold in the winter, at which the Lord gave me another idea. Remembering that when I visited my grandson, I always saw a big building with a big sign "YMCA." Finding out who was in charge, I made an appointment, and I thanked my Lord that I got permission to hold my Bible studies there.

I brought everything needed for a three-hour study those nights, including to start with our powerful "Jesus" film. The Large room had dozens of chairs already set up and the TV screen was enormous, to do our great film justice. It was unbelievable to me that these nights ended up with 20 to 35 Marines all three nights, depending which companies had returned those days.

64

This became my favorite ministry

Placing an advertisement and invitation on the bulletin board, asking my Savior to bring whom He wanted there and trusted Himim . On the first night only my grandson, his two buddies and one other Marine came and enjoyed it. The second study twelve appeared and from then on it was like a miracle. Twenty-five to thirty-five attended, pending which companies had gotten back that day.

Those three hours a night were gone in no time, and I left totally blessed, wanting to serve more. My Marines came to me asking if I could add a second night of Bible study, and I promised to ask. Well, I asked, and the YWCA representative said yes. We all thanked our Savior however I was not quite ready for a third night yet.

But guess what – my Marines came begging for just one more study night and guess what – I had the nerve to make another appointment. The one in charge was very kind and granted us a third night, but said that must be all, because they had their own programs the rest of the week. We all rejoiced and settled for three nights of three hours a night.

On the weekends I had permission to take my Bible students who were off, to my house for some getting to know God times and church. They were so grateful not having to go to the city with the rest of the students, where the temptations were very strong. At my house they felt free to ask questions they would not have in a larger group, and many had the same kind of broken homes as my youth from the Detention Center. So, our Savior did much healing.

Receiving dozens of letters from my soldiers when leaving for their permanent assignment was an award from my Savior. They were thanking God for having me there for them at this difficult training time. Having each of my Marines six months before they had to graduate and be transferred was a great lesson and blessing to me. They were calling me Mom because they considered me their spiritual mom, which helped with my empty nest pain.

64a The Lord's time for healing

One of my Marines was notified that his dad was in a fight and got killed. He got a week's leave to go home and me and be with his mother and the rest of his family. Coming back heart broken he hugged me and shared crying that his mom was so torn up that he never even got to talk with her.

Making sure that there was extra time to spend with him after the lesson was a blessing. He had a chance to pore out his heart. Telling him of God's deep and endless love gave the Counselor living in him the chance to calm him down. He told me how grateful he was for my being there for him and I told him that thanks need to go to our Lord who had sent me there. The Holy Spirit began His healing in him, and we had two more months before he left for his next assignment.

He wrote me an awesome farewell letter, as did most of my spiritual sons when they left this base. Having stacks of them, whenever Satan tries to get me down, I read a few of them out loud to him. And this enemy flees as it says in James 4:7, "submit to God, resist the Devil and he will flee from you."

Never would I have imagined all this when I first surrendered my life to the Lord my God. These young men, and I had thousands of them, said I was their spiritual mom, and called me mom. This truly helped me in missing my own, temporarily faraway sons. The YMCA room had an enormously big TV and whenever I had new Marines, I would show the "Jesus Film" of Campus Crusade, which was such a blessing.

Whenever there were new soldiers attending, I would give the Salvation prayer for the chance of them coming to the Lord. They loved to hear their Saviors promise, five times in the Old Testament and New Testament "I will never leave them or forsake them." This was such a great promise to keep on their mind as they left for their next assignment.

64b   Longing to share about this Salvation

Being overseas sixty-three times in twenty-seven countries, gave me a whole new vision of all the ones Jesus Christ died for. It also made me long to be used by Him to bring Him so many more to be saved. My merciful Savior God wanted me to choose Him and never to separate from Him, but also tell others His good news.

Many of the people I met had already found Him and lived with joy even in great trials. Like me, they looked forward to the promised, beautiful beginning of that new life without end. Just like the believers here at home, they were able to bear the temporary troubles or pain in this life, for the joy and beauty promised in the life to come.

Any suffering in this world, the Bible says, is nothing compared to the indescribable happiness in our eternal one. The believers in those countries trust and know about this promised eternal life with their Savior, written in the Bible we have given them. There were always Bible studies set up for these new believers to grow.

This came not only by experiencing His loving faithfulness but by spending much time in His precious letter to us. The Bible is the most valuable treasure to His children and covers every subject that will come up in their lives. I can vouch for this, having lived forty-eight years in total dependance of this merciful God.

Having seen His work of love not only in mine and my children's lives, but in thousands of those who learned to love and trust Him. I am eternally grateful for that blessed yet partial revelation of my Creators plan but will see it all when I am face to face with Him as promised.

65

Stir up your gift from God

This really touched my heart because I did not want to become lukewarm in the commitment I had made to my Savior. My wanting to be used meant doing my part of serving Him by reaching others who were seeking Him. I kept reminding myself of 2 Timothy 1:7 saying," for God has not given us a spirit of fear, but of power and of love and of a sound mind."

To me that meant I can securely live by what my beloved Father said is the truth. That also meant to me that I will seek from His word how to live and the things I need to avoid. It meant to keep in mind the beautiful promises like 2 Timothy 1:9 "God who saved us and called us with a holy calling, not according to our works, but according to His own purpose and grace, which was given to us in Christ Jesus before time began."

Again, I had to read this many times to catch all of this awesome promise. I love that it says He called us with a holy calling before time began, so we could not have earned anything. It is so hard to comprehend that it was before time began because that's when the world was created.

Just like the plan for Jesus' death and resurrection was planned before the world was started and He knew us and chose us then according to Ephesians 1:4 and 5. Well, I guess I will have to wait for this all to be revealed when I get to my eternal home and have a new body and mind.

Jesus himself said in John 16:12 "I still have many things to say to you, but you cannot bear them now." When the Holy Spirit came, He has guided us into all truth and has told us of things to come. There will be no end of our learning about this awesome God, who created it all.

66

Unlike His creation, only He knows the end.

The other scripture I love is when it mentions in Ephesians 1: 4 & 5, "just as He (the Father), chose us in Him (Jesus), before the foundation of the world, that we should be holy and without blame before Him in love." It is so amazing what took place before our God started to make it all and made it according to His great imagination. I think it was wonderfully and lovingly thought out before He began to create.

It is so awesome to relive my Fathers plan for me to this point and share His great love, faithfulness, and protection. Never having imagined writing it all down for you, it was an unbelievable joy. Trusting Him is the blessed secret of letting it happen His way without interfering.

When my Creator said in Romans 8:28 "All things work together for good to those who love God, to those who are the called according to His purpose." I had to stop and consider this promise. Since I truly love my God, this meant that all He has done in my life turned out for good, no matter how it seemed at the time. This says that even my painful experiences were allowed for His purpose in me.

I, then must admit, that it was all worth it, and none of that learning time was waisted because I got to know this awesome God. Now I can think of His past instructions in a new way and continue walking with Him in confidence knowing that He will never change. Jesus prayed to the Father for us, saying in John 17:17, "Sanctify them by Your truth, your word is truth. As You sent Me into the world, I also send them into the world."

Being sent into the world is an awesome adventure, what I learned could never have happened in other ways. Just to realize the amount and the variety of creations and the different ways they respond to His love. Even all the interpreters, if they were not believers when we arrived, they were by the time we left. It was an overwhelming joy. It is a never to be forgotten privilege to have experienced it and now being able to share it and encourage others.

67

What does meekness mean

The meek are believers who can submit to their God without arguing or resisting Him. It says in Matthew 5:5 "blessed are the meek," and it does not mean being passive. I agree with the comment that meek is not weak, but it is power under control. I would have to be strong and sure of who my Savior says I am, in order not to always be offended when someone talks down to me.

I continue to ask my beloved Lord to keep me humble because a short temper has always been part of my character which meant I had to do a lot of apologizing. That also meant I did not look as intelligent as I would have liked to, but instead was an embarrassment. But my merciful God helped me with this greatly and led me to memorize that the above verse continues saying, "for they shall inherit the earth."

It was a great joy when I could be humble and not give my enemy the joy of saying "all right she blew it again" but instead threw my future bridegroom a spiritual kiss. Being grateful that only one of my children inherited a bad temper allowed me to help him as my Lord helped me. Passing on my blessed lessons has always been a great joy to me and has given me a few of my rewards before I got to my eternal home.

After starting to write my books, my Creator showed me Habakuk 2:2 which says: "Write the vision and make it plain on tablets, that he may run who reads it." I took that as instructions from my Beloved and made that which I shared as clear as I could. That is why I always made sure that my words agreed with what He had written down in His letter to the children He loves so much, and not my own ideas.

Walking with my Savior has been an unbelievable adventure, something I would never have expected. This God I came to know is the most powerful and yet loving being in all of heaven and earth and I get to spend eternity with Him and all my brothers and sisters.

68

Only the Creator knows our new beginning.

Well, I am ready to close book number seven and see what my God has next for me. It is such a peace and no fear because I can vouch for His faithfulness, and nothing stops or changes unless He says so. This is what it promises in Psalms 33:4, 9, 11, "For the word of the Lord is right, and His work is done in truth. For He spoke and it was done, He commanded, and it stood fast. The counsel of the Lord stands forever, the plans of His heart to all generations."

Even though these past trips overseas or the ones in this country, are not all my beloved God has done in my life, but it has been so fun to relive what that precious Holy Spirit brought back to mind. There are no adventures I had to leave out because my Lord never gave me more than I could handle and always gave me a way of escape when needed.

This Creator of heaven and earth is in full control of every situation in His children's lives. I cannot wait to see all God has in store for the children He loves and that love Him in return. His Son has been working on homes for us and has much more to tell us once we are with Him.

How can I possibly deny and reject someone Who loves me this much. This life is so short in comparison to all eternity, and what I love best is that we will not sin and offend Him anymore then. Hallelujah!

Jesus gave me my gifts so we can enjoy them together. Did I do what He told me and called me for? Did I try to copy others and miss His voice and directions? Did I sometimes do things my way and ask Him to bless it? Whatever was not done perfectly has been corrected and forgiven and I learned from my mistakes.

*Is it n*ot wonderful that I was invited to come to my Savior at times like this and say "help, I am sorry, only You can fix this" and patiently wait for the solution for wrong choices. He will pick it up, and in His perfect way will restore it to what it should have been in the very beginning and for His purpose. He will continue His loving work of making me into the person He always wanted me to be. Remembering that He knew me before creation, I looked up Ephesians 1:4 and 5 for reference where it tells us that the Father chose us in Jesus before the foundations of the world.

69

The good pleasure of His will.

He continues telling us that He did this so we would be holy and without blame before Him in love, having predestined us as sons by Jesus Christ to Himself, according to the good pleasure of His will. Our beloved merciful Creator knew that we would mess up, but He created us anyway. He also knew that He would finish the work He began in us, and we would be perfect by the time He came to take us home.

Our faithful Creator never gets tired of inviting us to come to Him because we are forgiven, and He will keep us on the high road. Violent storms bring hopefulness, but the self-effort of Paul's companions could not keep the boat together. Christians will try to bail out when things at church do not agree with them and leave for another place. It is important to love and support the body of Christ which the Savior has led them to and not let the enemy take over.

This would not be the time to leave the church or the marriage or relationship or job. This would be the time to trust the One who delivered and saved them for all eternity. We are encouraged to take what God has already provided, and not come up with our own solutions. Desiring His purposes and wanting to encourage others was my reason for the writings and I know it was His also. Having all my life enjoyed God's creations made it increase greatly when e entered itmy beloved Redeemer had entered it.

I had a dear friend my age and when we had time, we would go up to the mountains and praise our God and admire His fantastic imagination. Well, my friend has gone to be with our Lord recently, but when we are back together in heaven, we can enjoy all even more and tell our Lord so face to face. This is what Jesus said we will do when we are with Him. I shared with you most of what the Holy Spirit brought to my remembrance. I feel there is more to come and If God wants, I will share that with you also, with love and prayers for you, Hannah.

"Have you heard about the Four Spiritual Laws"

www.ingramcontent.com/pod-product-compliance
Lightning Source LLC
Chambersburg PA
CBHW061737070526
44585CB00024B/2711